Estate Planning

for California Residents

by Milton Berry Scott

CCH INCORPORATED
Chicago

A WoltersKluwer Company

Editorial Staff

Production . . . . Christopher Zwirek

Index . . . . Lynn Brown

ISBN 0-8080-1091-3

Preface

Why a specialized book for the State of California? California is one of nine community property states and because of the nature of community property, estate planning in a community property state is quite different from the other 41 states. Community property law allows husband and wife to each own an equal interest in community property assets and makes estate planning in terms of trusts and other estate planning techniques much simpler than in non-community property states. In addition, upon the death of either husband or wife, *all* of the couple's community property assets get a new valuation for income tax purposes. This is obviously extremely beneficial for income tax purposes.

Most estate planning books try to address the estate planning process throughout the United States, with only a reference to, or separate chapter for community property rules. The few books that address California estate planning either are very simple texts or very large and complicated legal tomes.

This book is a concise guide to California estate planning. It helps the reader understand the legal issues without extensive detail. It explains the law in simple terms and serves to direct those who need more detail.

When this book was written nearly two decades ago it was designed for the general public as well as attorneys and other professionals in the estate planning field. This third edition serves the same audience and is thoroughly revised to reflects the various legal and tax developments that have taken place since the second edition published in 1996.

The first edition of this book was published in 1985 and estate planning has changed dramatically in the 19 years that followed. The federal estate tax exemption, which was $500,000 in 1985, increased only to $600,000 in the years 1987 through 1998. In 1998 the estate tax exemption was increased over a period of years to $1,000,000. Then, in 2001, Congress again increased the exemption, in steps to $3,500,000 in 2009. The estate tax is now due to disappear in 2010 and, unless Congress votes to change it, will be reinstated in 2011 with a $1,000,000 exemption.

Income tax rates and capital gains tax rates have changed numerous times. California annually makes many changes in the California Probate Code affecting estate planning, probate procedures, and trusts. Nothing is certain, and nothing is permanent. Taxpayers and their advisers must keep abreast of these changes and review their estate plans (wills, trusts, powers of attorney, etc.) to determine if changes must be made.

Designed as a book that can be used by practitioners as well as those who are not experts on California estate planning, minor exceptions and points have been omitted. Major points and major exceptions are the focus.

Many publications attempt to be do-it-yourself books, sometimes with sample wills and trusts documents. This book is not that type. People who attempt to do their own estate planning without professional assistance or advice are asking for difficulty later. This book is intended to give the reader a basic working knowledge of the field so that one see how it generally applies to individual situations. If the reader is not a practitioner, her or she can intelligently talk to an attorney, accountant, financial planner or other professional about what should be done. This should save the reader time with the professional who will not have to explain the basics of estate planning. For practitioners, the book offers a concise quick study on the major points and considerations in California estate planning.

Since the federal government and the State of California annually change tax and estate planning laws, a book is only useful if it is up to date. This book covers all federal and California law changes as of December 31, 2003.

Milton Berry Scott

January 2004

About the Author

Milton Berry Scott is an attorney with over 30 years experience whose practice focuses on trust planning, probate, charitable giving, and complex estate planning. He is certified by the California Board of Legal Specialization of the State Bar of California as a specialist in probate, estate planning, and trust law. He served as an instructor in the paralegal program at St. Mary's College for 16 years. He is a frequent speaker at estate planning councils, real estate programs, financial planning conferences, charitable giving seminars, CPA programs and enrolled agent meetings. Scott is the author of two other helpful books, Probate in California and What to Do When Someone Dies: A Legal, Financial, and Practical Guide.

Acknowledgements

An acknowledgment should be made to my son, Jeff Scott, and my wife, Marilyn, who have assisted me with a very critical eye in terms of style and also given me assistance in terms of looking at this subject from a layperson's point of view.

Table of Contents

Chapter 1

ESTATE PLANNING

¶101 What is Estate Planning?

Estate planning is the planning of the disposition of an individual's assets, both at death and during that individual's lifetime. It includes deciding whom will receive various assets upon death, determining what potential estate taxes and probate costs will be, and establishing a plan to accomplish the decedent's wishes and reduce the estate taxes and probate costs.

The death of a loved one is a difficult and emotional experience. The last thing someone wants to deal with is the legal and financial complexities that may arise because the decedent failed to do adequate planning before death. Planning the estate reduces the complexities, hassle, costs and difficulties for the survivors.

Estate planning is more than the drafting of a will. In planning, one must also review the title to assets; check beneficiary designations of life insurance and employee benefits; determine the estimated estate taxes and costs at death; and consider how these taxes and costs can be reduced or eliminated.

Estate planning involves time, details, and decisions. Alternates must be examined and documents must be drafted. Too often people want their estate plan completed before they fly off on vacation in a few days. While it is possible to draft a will and have it executed in a few hours, it takes time to evaluate ones assets and decide how one would wish to dispose of these assets at death. The time involved may take from a few days to several months, depending on the nature of the assets and the type of estate plan.

Too often, a planner is phoned by a client's spouse or child from the hospital. The spouse or parent may have talked about a living trust but never had it prepared. Now, after a stroke or heart attack, he or she wants it immediately. In some cases the person requires serious surgery in a few hours or the next day. Because of time constraints, it is impossible to draft a complex estate plan. It would have been far better if the person had prepared the estate plan months or years earlier, when he first discussed it with the planner.

Attention to detail is necessary in reviewing and examining documents such as deeds to real estate, title on stock certificates, beneficiary designations for life insurance, IRA and other employee benefits. If changes are needed, it might be necessary to change title to various assets owned and beneficiary designations for life insurance and other benefits. Very often people pass over these details and then after death, survivors must deal with unintended results.

Decisions are required. Who gets the assets? Who should get the furniture and furnishings? Who will be the executor, trustee, guardian for minor children? At what ages should the young children receive the assets? All of these questions require answers. Some people seem incapable making the necessary decisions, and nothing ever gets prepared. Experienced planners know that it is better to make decisions based on current facts and then modify your plan by amendment later, rather than do nothing now.

¶102 Reviewing Assets

Everyone has an estate plan whether they know it or not. If one does not prepare a plan, the State of California makes one, providing who will inherit the present estate plan assets.

.01 Systematic, Organized Review

Many people rush into an estate planning interview with an attorney without any preparation. When the attorney asks how the individual or couple hold title to assets such as the home, the client often doesn't know. The client sometimes hasn't given thought to an executor for his will and must have to think about it.

To do any estate planning, organization is a must. A detailed list of assets is needed; a bank loan statement lists much of the information. Separate listings for real estate, securities, bank and savings and loan accounts, life insurance, employee benefits, and other assets are needed. An attempt to do this in the attorney's waiting room, or any time right before a meeting, will not be successful.

The old saying, "nothing is certain but death and taxes" is especially true in estate planning. Many people speak of their death, as "if I die." It is not a question of "if I die," but "when I die."

.02 Value of Assets

One very important concern is to estimate the current fair market value of the various assets owned by an individual. With this information the attorney can estimate any estate taxes due at your death and talk about ways of reducing or eliminating the taxes. The federal estate tax structure has changed dramatically in the last few years. The estate tax exemption, which was $600,000 several years ago, has increased to $1,500,000 in 2004, and is due to increase significantly in the next few years. If the individual or couple has less than the exemption, no estate tax is due after death and planning becomes much simpler. However, if the estate will be over this exemption, then planning becomes important.

Exact value is not important but it is possible to estimate values. Whether the home is worth $480,000, $500,000 or $520,000 is not important. Whether it is worth $500,000 or $800,000 is very important. Most people have a general idea of the worth of their home and other real estate. They also know the approximate value of their stock and various mutual funds. Money in the bank, face amount of life insurance and the value of IRA, Keogh and other retirement accounts at death are generally easily ascertainable.

The attorney needs a rough estimate, knowing whether an estate is worth $400,000, $800,000 or $2,000,000, an attorney can then intelligently discuss death taxes and possible estate planning techniques to reduce these taxes.

.03 Title to Assets and Beneficiary Designations

One of the most important aspects of estate planning is to determine how title is held to the various assets: real estate, securities, mutual funds, brokerage accounts, bank accounts, U.S. Savings bonds, cars, etc.

Title can be taken by a husband and wife as joint tenants, community property, tenants in common, or in the name of either husband and wife alone. Each method has different legal and tax ramifications, which are explained in Chapter 3. In order to properly advise the individual or couple, it is necessary to accurately determine how title is held. This means checking deeds, stock certificates and other documents.

A planner interviewed a client and his wife, both in their 70s. The couple had assets scattered in a number of different forms of registration. Some of the assets were registered in the husband's name alone, some in the wife's name alone, and some in both of their names as joint tenants, as community property and even as tenants in common. After the meeting, the couple went home to review and make decisions regarding changes in title. But later in the day the husband suffered a heart attack and died that evening.

The husband left several handwritten wills with a variety of contradictory provisions, and not everything was left to the wife. The complications for the family are enormous. The probate could last for several years with very large legal fees. This could have been easily avoided by organizing title to the various assets so that they all passed in an organized way at death.

Certain assets, such as life insurance policies, annuities, individual retirement accounts, Keogh plans, corporate pension and profit-sharing plans, and 401(k) plans are controlled by the designated beneficiary, so the assets in these funds go to the person or persons named. A will or living trust does not control these types of assets. The assets go instead to the person designated as the beneficiary. The beneficiary designation supersedes the will.

Who is the beneficiary? Many times the individual has filled out a form when he or she opened an IRA account or took out a life insurance policy many years ago. Frequently the person does not have a copy of the beneficiary designation. Instead of checking with the institution involved, the person guesses as to who the beneficiary of the plan is and sometimes after death it turns out that the guess was incorrect.

.04 Other Considerations

Are there special considerations in drafting the estate plan? Is one of the children handicapped and unable to manage the assets if he or she inherits a share? Is one of the children a "spendthrift" who cannot manage funds? Does one wish a portion of the estate to go to grandchildren who are minors?

Many families have problems in terms of not being able to leave everything equally to the children. In addition to other issues, it is important to set up a person's estate plan to take into account these special needs. In many cases, a portion of the assets may have to stay in trust for the lifetime of a child or grandchild. Terms of the trust, who inherits the assets when the child dies, and who is going to be the trustee and manage the assets, are all questions that must be answered.

¶103 Evaluating the Estate Plan

Before undertaking any planning, it is important to look at the existing plan, as poor as it may be. Everyone has an estate plan, if one does not make a will, a person is considered to die "intestate," and the State of California determines who gets the assets.

.01 Who Gets Assets at Death?

It is necessary to evaluate who inherits the assets. Most people look at the will, but in many cases the will controls little or no assets at death.

Who is listed as the beneficiary on life insurance, annuities, employee benefits, and other assets where you can name a beneficiary? What assets are in joint tenancy and who are the other joint tenants? Do one have a living trust? If so, who are the beneficiaries of the trust and who are the successor trustees to manage the trust?

Who is listed in the will or living trust to inherit? Who are the alternate beneficiaries if the primary beneficiary dies? Do the children of a deceased child inherit if a child dies ahead of the parent?

Not infrequently a planner may have a couple whom wish to revise a will which may be 10-15 years old. In doing so, it may be discovered that a former attorney or friend, whom they have not heard from in years, is the trustee, executor, and guardian for minor children if both husband and wife die. The couple believes that to be incorrect. But upon reading a copy of the will, they realize they have not read the will since they signed it many years ago, and it is completely out of date.

.02 Estimated Death Taxes and Probate Costs

What will be the estimated estate tax at the death of either spouse and upon the death of the surviving spouse? If the individual or couple has over $1,500,000 to $3,500,000, depending upon the year of death, there most likely will be a tax due. With the estate tax rates currently starting at 45% and rising to a maximum of 45-48%, estimating values is very important. For estate tax purposes, the government taxes everything the decedent owned including life insurance and employee benefits.

An individual will not conserve taxes by attempting to underestimate the value of ones estate. The federal government bases its tax on the "fair market value" of all of the decedent's assets. An individual needs to estimate the current value of all of their assets. With an estimate of the potential taxes, it is then possible to look at some of the ways to reduce or eliminate these taxes.

"Probate" is a legal process that may occur at death. It has no relationship to "estate taxes." The federal government taxes assets whether they go through this probate process or not. Avoiding probate does not avoid estate taxes.

A "will" is a legal document directing who inherits the assets that one owns and which go through the probate process. Many people confuse making a will with the avoidance of probate. Assets may go through probate whether there is a will or not.

Most people want to avoid probate. What assets are subject to the probate process? In California, if the value of the assets which would go through the probate process are under $100,000, probate may be avoided. If they are over this amount, all of the assets in the decedent's name alone are probated.

In California, the executor or administrator and the attorney each receive a "statutory" or fixed fee set by law. This is based on the value of the assets that go through the probate process. The fee amounts to approximately 2-4% for each party, or a total of 4-8% if both parties take a fee. The attorney and executor can also each request additional or "extraordinary" compensation for special services rendered.

.03 Disability

Estate planning usually means planning for death. However, it also includes planning for incapacity. What happens if one suffers a stroke and cannot sign their name or manage their assets? Does someone else have a durable power of attorney for management purposes? If not, it may be necessary to go through a court proceedings called a "conservatorship." This is a legal proceeding that is more involved than probate. To avoid a conservatorship, one can set up assets in a living trust, put bank accounts in joint tenancy, and have a durable power of attorney.

In addition to the management of assets, who makes health care decisions? Does an individual wish to be kept on a life support system? To avoid problems, one also needs to execute a durable power of attorney for health care. This document names an agent to make these decisions if one cannot do so. It also gives the agent directions on how to handle these decisions.

¶104 Creating a New Estate Plan

After an individual reviews the assets he or she owns, they should determine who inherits these assets, what the estate taxes and probate costs will be and who will manage assets in the case of disability. A decision must be made as to what changes, if any, one wishes to make. Does the individual want to establish a living trust or draft powers of attorney?

.01 Will

A will is a cornerstone of an estate plan. It is important that the will be tied in with other provisions of the plan. If the person or couple has set up a living trust, then a will with "pour-over" provisions, adding any assets missed at death to the living trust, should probably be used. The will should reflect who inherits the person's property and who will be the executor or executrix to manage the assets and undertake the probate proceedings at death. It may be a short document of two or three pages, or may be very extensive, covering 20-30 pages.

While it is possible to do a handwritten will, which is legal in California, or complete a form purchased from a service or stationery store, an attorney should be used since mistakes in self-drafting are frequent and will not be discovered until after death. It is far better to do it right and pay an attorney to be sure it is correct rather than have problems after death. It is better to pay an attorney $400-1,000 to do the will correctly, rather than pay $5,000-20,000 to correct everything that was done wrong by doing it oneself.

A planner deals with many handwritten wills and self-drafted wills after a death has occurred. Many require involved court proceedings and costs that were higher than if an attorney just drafted the will. For example, a man wants his adult granddaughter to receive a note secured by deed of trust of approximately $100,000 when he dies. Rather than put this in the will or make a codicil to his will, he merely took the original note, types on it that he wants it to go to his granddaughter at death and signs it.

At his death the question arises as to whether this statement was a will and passed the note to his granddaughter. Since this was typed and not in his handwriting it was not a holographic or handwritten will. Since it was not witnessed, it was not a witnessed will. The court must hold that the typed provisions were invalid and the note passed by the decedent's will to other relatives. The granddaughter doesn't get the $100,000 note.

.02 Living Trust Agreement

Many people and couples use a living trust agreement or declaration. Such a document avoids the probate process, solves many of the legal problems associated with incapacity, and for a couple, can significantly reduce or eliminate the estate tax. A living trust is not for everyone and in many cases is "oversold," but it should be considered by everyone to see whether it fits that person's estate plan.

Merely signing a living trust is not sufficient. It is necessary to reregister most assets in the name of the trustee of the trust and to change the beneficiary designation for many other assets.

.03 Powers of Attorney

A will takes effect at death. A living trust solves some problems in connection with incapacity but does not avoid all potential problems. A person should also execute a general durable power of attorney. This power of attorney gives someone the right to act for the person in terms of signing legal documents and handling legal matters. It can either be effective immediately, giving the person selected (one's "agent") very broad authority, or it may be a "springing" power of attorney that only comes into being on one's legal incapacity.

This power of attorney covers the signing of income tax returns, medical claim forms, and various other legal matters. Even with a living trust, a power of attorney may be needed to handle assets that are not in the living trust.

A durable power of attorney for health care is a legally recognized document in California. It gives the person selected the right to make health care decisions only if one is not able to do so. The agent selected may examine medical records and consent or not consent to medical treatment. It will also allow an individual to be taken off a life support system or not put onto such a system if one is terminally ill and there is no reasonable hope of recovery. If a person does not sign such a document, then the nearest relatives will jointly have the right to make these decisions.

.04 Gifts

A properly drafted living trust can protect up to $3,000,000 or a larger amount, depending upon the year of death, from taxes for husband and wife. If the person is not married, the exemption is only $1,500,000. What if the person or couple has assets with a greater value?

Federal tax law allows people to make gifts each year. These gifts are then out of the decedent's estate at death and are not taxed for estate tax purposes. If one gives $11,000 per year to an only child for six years prior to death, a total of $66,000 has been given. Had the gift not been made and subject to estate tax at the minimum rate of 45% at death, the additional tax at death would have been $29,700. The child gets the additional $29,700 instead of the Internal Revenue Service.

Gifts are nearly always beneficial and save taxes. Unfortunately, for many reasons people do not make gifts before death, or if they make gifts, they fail to give the maximum amount. As a result, the federal government gets a larger estate tax.

.05 Change in Title to Assets and Beneficiary Designations

After reviewing how the individual or couple holds title to assets it may be necessary to change title. This may involve changing title to the living trust, changing from joint tenancy to community property, removing a joint tenant, or other changes.

Change in title frequently involves recording a deed or deeds to change title to real property, contacting a local brokerage firm to change title to a brokerage account, physically sending in stock and bond certificates to have the names changed, or taking other action to change title. Change in title is very involved and takes time, but it can be very important by saving significant taxes after death.

Because of the hassle, time, and complexities involved, many people do not change title. A planner often discusses changes in title with their clients and also writes them about doing so, but often many years later when the client has died, he or she still never got around to doing this.

Along with a possible change in title, it is frequently necessary to change the beneficiary designation of life insurance, an IRA account, and other types of assets.

Who should be the beneficiary? In most cases there should also be a secondary beneficiary in the event the primary beneficiary is deceased. If the husband names the wife as the only beneficiary of his $150,000 life insurance policy and she has died ahead of him, then at his death this $150,000 will have to be probated because there is no beneficiary. If he had named his children equally as the secondary beneficiaries, they would have received these funds without probate.

Who the primary and secondary beneficiaries should be depends upon the estate plan. It also depends upon the nature of the asset. A life insurance policy is subject to estate tax but not to income tax. If a couple sets up a living trust, the life insurance beneficiary usually should be changed to name the trust as the primary beneficiary.

If the husband has a large IRA rollover account, this is subject to estate tax *and* income tax, with special income tax provisions for the wife. If the couple has a living trust, they may not wish the beneficiary to be the trust, but may want to name the wife as the primary beneficiary and the children equally as the secondary beneficiaries.

There is no automatic rule as to who should be the beneficiary. It, like other things, depends upon the nature of the person's estate plan.

¶105 Carrying Out the New Estate Plan

It is important to make decisions as to what to do in connection with an estate plan. However, no matter how good the intentions, one must physically sign all of the documents necessary to carry out the plan. If one dies without signing them, they are not legal.

For example, a planner interviewed a couple in late November regarding their assets. They had an estate of approximately $2,400,000. Because of the size of the estate, they decided to draft a living trust, which would save approximately $500,000 in probate costs and estate taxes.

The planner drafted the documents and sent them to the couple in approximately two weeks. The following February the planner wrote them regarding the signing of the documents. The wife phoned and said that the husband had been ill and that they would be in to see the planner when the husband was better. In late August they made an appointment, but before the appointment, the husband had a heart attack and died. Everything went to the wife. Although the wife later set up a living trust to avoid probate at her death, she now owns all of the couple's $2,400,000 assets. When the wife dies, her estate will pay an additional $400,000 in estate taxes because the husband did not sign the trust prior to death.

Planners find many clients decide on an estate plan, have documents drafted and then never get around to signing anything. After having made the decision, a planner is confused as to why a client cannot come in to sign the documents and get the plan set up.

Planners also find that on occasion, a couple will come back five to ten years after a will or a living trust has been drafted. In many cases the planner has not retained copies of the drafted documents and must start over again.

If a will or living trust is not the way the person wishes it, it needs to be changed. If it is correct, then it needs to be signed.

¶106 Periodic Review

Once an individual or a couple sign all of the required documents and change title and beneficiary designation, they then breath a sigh of relief, place everything in the safe deposit box, and do their best to forget it. But, an estate plan is only as good as it is up to date.

Legal or tax considerations require changes in the plan. In 1981, Congress allowed a spouse to leave his or her estate of any value to the other spouse tax free at death. However, if a trust was involved, in order to get the increased deduction, the trust had to be amended. Hundreds of thousands of trusts had to be changed.

In 1988 Congress changed the same law, so that a person could not leave their estate tax free to a spouse if it was more than $600,000 and if the spouse was not a United States citizen. A special type of trust had to be used.

Both of these legal changes required most wills and trusts to be amended.

An individual or couple may want to change the trustee or executor, change ages for distribution for children, or "lock up" a child's share because they have come to the conclusion that the child cannot manage the inheritance.

Like other things in life, change is inevitable. An estate plan should be reread and thoroughly reviewed every two or three years. It also needs to be reviewed if there is a death in the family, a large inheritance, a move to another state or country, physical or mental incapacity of a party, or when other circumstances arise. It is usually relatively simple to draft a codicil to a will or amendment to a living trust, or to change the power of attorney.

From 2004 though 2011, the federal estate tax will change dramatically, as shown in Chapter 7.

California makes changes nearly every year regarding probate and estate planning. These changes do not affect everyone, but depending upon the changes, they affect some people. Planners should try to advise clients on changes that they believe affects an estate plan.

Chapter 2

TITLE TO ASSETS

¶200 Introduction

One of the most important considerations in estate planning is how title is held to various assets. Real estate, stocks, bank accounts and other assets can be titled or registered in a variety of ways. How title is taken affects what happens to these assets at death. Most people ignore the importance of taking title to assets and initially register the assets in whatever title seems appropriate or convenient at the time.

¶201 Ways of Taking Title To Assets

There are a number of ways of taking title to assets. Title may be taken in an individual's name alone, in the name of two or more people as joint tenants, in the name of husband and wife as community property, in the name of husband and wife as community property with right of survivorship, in the name of two or more people as tenants in common, in a "trustee" designation, or "payable on death" or "transfer of death" designation with a named beneficiary or beneficiaries.

.01 Joint Tenancy

One way of holding title is in joint tenancy.[1] If an asset is held in joint tenancy, it passes at death to the surviving joint tenant or tenants and not by the decedent's will. The joint tenancy designation supersedes the decedent's will regarding the joint tenancy asset. Joint tenancy means "right of survivorship" even though these words do not appear on a deed or other document. Any two or more people, whether related or not, may hold virtually any asset, such as real estate, stocks, bank account, cars, or other property, in joint tenancy. There is no probate proceeding with regard to these assets at death.

Gift. One disadvantage of placing an asset in joint tenancy is that for some types of assets, merely placing it in joint tenancy makes it a taxable gift.[2] If Mary Doe adds her two children to the title of her home, each joint tenant has an equal interest. By adding her two children, she has given away two-thirds of her home. If the value of her home at the time of the gift is $600,000, then she has made a gift of $400,000. A gift tax return would be due at the end of the year.

Placing certain types of assets in joint tenancy is considered a gift. These types of assets would include real estate, stocks and bonds, mutual funds, and United States treasury bills and notes. The determination of whether the creation of a joint tenancy is a gift depends on whether the original owner can take the

---

[1] California Civil Code section 683.　　　　[2] Internal Revenue regulations 25-2511-1(h) (5).

asset out of joint tenancy without the other joint tenants' written approval. If the original owner cannot do this, then the creation of a joint tenancy is a gift.

It is not a gift to place or hold other assets in joint tenancy. These types of assets include bank and savings and loan accounts, brokerage accounts, United States savings bonds, and autos, boats and other vehicles registered under the California Vehicle Code.

If adding someone as a joint tenant creates a gift, then the income from the asset or on any gain, if the asset is sold, is taxable to the new joint tenant. If Mary Doe adds her two children to her home and then wants to sell the home, her children must join in the sale and are taxable on a portion of the gain. If the home is sold and Mary Doe wants to use her $250,000 capital gains exemption on the sale of her home, the exemption will only apply to her one-third of the proceeds of sale. Her two children will not be able to use the exemption.

In addition, if the creation of the joint tenancy is a gift, then the other joint tenants can transfer their shares of the asset and their creditors can reach that portion. Mary Doe adds her two children to her home as joint tenants. One child has a financial problem and decides to sell his portion of his mother's home (his one-third) to another party. He can legally do that, and the buyer would then own one-third of the home. If the son is sued and his creditors get a judgment against him, the creditors can force the sale of the home and take one-third of the proceeds of the sale. Since the son does not normally live in the home, he cannot homestead it.

Joint Tenancy Fully Taxed at Death. Even though the transfer of an asset into joint tenancy is considered a gift in some cases, it is still fully taxable at death.[3] Husband and wife are normally exempt from estate taxation. If the joint tenants are not husband and wife, the asset will be fully taxable at death. Mary Doe places her $600,000 home in joint tenancy with her two children. Even if she files a gift tax return, at her death the government will tax the full value of the home for estate tax purposes. Thus, the $600,000 value will be added to the value of all of her other assets. The fact that she is considered to own one-third of the home does not matter at her death. There are no estate tax savings, only the avoidance of the probate process. Conversely, if either of her children dies ahead of her, the value of the home will not be considered taxable in the child's estate because their mother is still considered the full owner for estate tax purposes.

Termination of Joint Tenancy at Death. To terminate joint tenancy at death, no legal proceeding is required. A certified copy of the deceased person's death certificate is all that is needed. For real property, a real estate form entitled "Affidavit-Death of Joint Tenant" is recorded with the county recorder. For other assets, the death certificate is provided the bank, brokerage firm or stock or bond transfer agent.

---

[3] Internal Revenue Code section 2040(a).

¶201.01

.02 Community Property

In California the term "community property" has two separate meanings. It can refer to assets acquired by husband and wife during marriage while living in California.[4] This is described in more detail in Chapter 3.

It also refers to a method of taking title to assets. In California husband and wife can take title to real estate, securities, bank accounts, or other assets in both of their names as "community property."[5] Unlike joint tenancy, each spouse may will away his or her one-half of each community property asset at death to anyone he or she wishes. The asset does not automatically pass to the surviving spouse.

If a married person wills away his or her half of a community property asset, it normally goes through probate.

If a married person dies without a will, under California laws regarding intestate succession, all community property assets pass entirely to the surviving spouse.[6]

If assets that are titled as community property pass to the surviving spouse by will or intestate succession, it is necessary in most cases to go through a court proceeding. California has abolished a probate proceedings for assets passing to the spouse, although a one-time court proceeding, called a "Spousal Confirmation Proceeding" is required,[7] and is discussed in Chapter 6. With a court order, the surviving spouse can transfer the community property assets into the survivor's name.

.03 Community Property with Right of Survivorship

Since 2001, California has allowed husband and wife to take title to real property as "community property with right of survivorship." This applies only to California real estate and not to other types of assets. The deed to the property must specifically state "community property with right of survivorship" and also have a statement on the deed signed by both spouses that they consent.

The advantage of this title registration is the couple gets a stepped up basis on the entire property for income tax purposes at the first death but does not have to go through a probate or spousal confirmation proceedings. At the first death, the surviving spouse can record a real estate form entitled "Affidavit-Death of Surviving Spouse with Right of Survivorship."[8]

.04 Tenants in Common

Several people as "tenants in common" may hold a few assets, mostly real estate. This means that each person owns an undivided interest in the asset.[9] At death, this interest does not pass to the other owners, but is instead controlled by the deceased person's will. The interests do not have to be equal interests, as they do in joint tenancy.

---

[4] California Probate Code section 28.
[5] California Family Code section 760.
[6] California Probate Code section 6401(a).

[7] California Probate Code sections 13650-13660.
[8] California Civil Code section 682.
[9] California Civil Code section 685.

For real estate, the term "tenants in common" is not used. Instead the term "undivided interest" appears on the deed. A deed may show property in the name of John Doe as to an undivided 30% interest, Frank Smith as to an undivided 50% interest, and Martha Smith as to an undivided 20% interest. The parties are tenants in common and each can pass his or her share of the property at death by his or her will.

.05 Individual Name

It is possible to take title in the sole name of one individual, whether married or not. A parcel or real estate may be in the name of "John Doe, a married man."

If the person is not married, the decedent's will or the rules of intestate succession apply regarding who inherits the asset.

If the decedent is married, then it is necessary to carefully review how the property was acquired. It is possible for community property to be held in the name of either spouse alone. Merely titling an asset in a person's name alone does not necessarily make it separate property.

If the asset is community property, then one-half of that asset passes by the deceased spouse's will, and the other half must go to the surviving spouse. If the asset was acquired by the deceased spouse before marriage or during marriage as a gift or as inheritance, then the asset is that person's separate property. A person may will away all of his or her separate property at death and is not required to leave any of this separate property to the surviving spouse.

.06 Tenants by the Entireties

There is a special type of joint tenancy referred to as "tenants by the entireties." This is nothing more than a joint tenancy between husband and wife. California does not recognize this type of registration, but it is used in many states.

.07 Trustee Registration

It is possible to register bank, savings association, and credit union accounts in a "trustee" registration. There is no written trust or other document. The account is registered in a person's name as trustee for another. An account may be in the name of "John Doe, Trustee for Frank Doe." The money in the account belongs to John Doe and he can withdraw the funds at any time. John Doe receives any interest on the account and pays income tax on the interest received. At the death of John Doe, the account balance does not pass by the will but goes to the named beneficiary; Frank Doe.[10] No probate is required. Although Frank Doe has no access to the account while John Doe is alive, he only needs a death certificate to obtain the funds at death.

It is possible to have the account set up in two names as trustees for someone. An account could be in the name of "John Doe and Mary Doe, Trustees for Frank Doe." At the death of John Doe the account is treated as a joint tenancy account and passes to Mary Doe. At the death of Mary Doe, if she has not changed the title on the account, it passes to Frank Doe.

---

[10] California Probate Code section 5404.

¶201.05

It is also possible to name several beneficiaries for an account. The account may be titled in the name of "John Doe, Trustee for Frank Doe, Mary Doe, and Martha Smith." When John Doe dies, the three named beneficiaries divide the money in the account equally.

This trustee account cannot be used for securities or real property, but only for an account at a financial institution.

Many financial institutions abbreviate this type of account as "ATF," which stands for "as trustee for."

.08 Payable on Death Registration

Some assets may be registered in a person's name so that they are "payable on death" to a named beneficiary. Occasionally this is abbreviated "P.O.D."

This type of registration can be used for bank, savings association, and credit union accounts. It is very similar to a trustee registration. It may also be used for United States savings bonds and for vehicles registered under the California Vehicle Code. For bank and other accounts, several people may be named as beneficiaries. For United States savings bonds and vehicles, only one beneficiary may be named.

If an account or the registration is in the name of "John Doe P.O.D. Frank Doe" the asset belongs to and is legally controlled exclusively by John Doe during his lifetime. At his death, Frank Doe inherits the asset and needs only a certified copy of the death certificate to change title.[11]

This type of registration avoids probate and supersedes the individual's will.

.09 Transfer on Death Registration

Since 1999, California has allowed securities to be registered in a "T.O.D." registration, which stands for "Transfer on Death." This is similar to a P.O.D. registration for bank accounts. Such registration covers individual securities, brokerage accounts, reinvestment accounts, mutual funds, and other forms of securities. Such a registration is only allowed if the brokerage firm, transfer agent, mutual fund, or transfer agency permits it.

Like a P.O.D. account, this registration avoids probate and supersedes the individual's will

The securities or account may be registered using the term "T.O.D." or the words "Transfer on Death." The registration of an account as "John Doe, T.O.D. Frank Doe" can be used where John Doe owns the account and wishes it to go to his son, Frank Doe at death.

A registration can be designated naming multiple beneficiaries or successor beneficiaries. An account can be in joint tenancy with a beneficiary named to receive the account upon the death of both joint tenants.[12]

---

[11] California Probate Code section 5403.   [12] California Probate Code sections 5500-5512.

¶202 Determining How Title Is Held

It is important to know how title to assets is held. This means checking the documents, such as the deed for real estate or stock certificates. Many people merely guess how title is held and after death, it is discovered that the title should have been in another registration. It is then too late, and complications, probate, and estate taxes may all be increased. It is necessary to look at the following documents to determine the registration of the asset.

.01 Real Property

The deed, which was recorded with the county recorder when the property was purchased, will list the name of the party or parties who purchased the property and how they hold title. Title may be in the name of husband and wife as community property, or in two or more names as joint tenants or tenants in common, or in another designation. If there has been a refinancing of the property or a change in title, the last deed should be examined.

.02 Deed of Trust

The deed of trust for which money has been lent shows the name or names of the "beneficiary" and indicates how title is held. Title can be held in the same registration as real property.

.03 Note

A note covers money lent and indicates the name or names of the lender. If it lists two or more people, it should show how they hold title. The note may be unsecured, or it may be secured by the deed of trust, which places a lien on the real estate of the borrower. Title can also be held the same manner as real property.

.04 Registered Stocks and Bonds

Stock and bond certificates are either in an individual's name or in the names of two or more people. If it's in the names of two or more people, the certificates indicate "JTWROS" which stands for "joint tenants with right of survivorship, "JT TEN" which stands for joint tenancy, "COMM PROP" which means husband and wife holding title as community property, or "TEN COMM" which stands for tenants in common.

.05 Stock Brokerage Account

An account with a brokerage firm can be registered the same way as stock or bond certificates. The brokerage firm normally holds the certificates. The title on the brokerage account governs all securities and other assets held in this account. The monthly statement on the account should show how title is held.

.06 Mutual Fund

When mutual funds are purchased, no certificates are generally issued by the fund. A statement similar to a stock brokerage account is issued periodically. Title to the mutual fund is shown on the mutual fund statement and is similar to stock registration.

.07 Stock Reinvestment Plan Shares

The shares that are purchased under a stock reinvestment account are registered the same way as the underlining stock certificates. The statement issued quarterly by the stock purchase agent shows how the account is registered.

.08 United States Treasury Obligations

Treasury obligations may be taken in a single name or in the name of two people (but not more than two people) as joint tenants, community property, or tenants in common. The term "or" means that it is joint tenancy. If individual bonds are held, which is rare, the bond will show how title is held. If the obligations are purchased under a treasury direct account, the statement for the account will show how title is held.

.09 United States Savings Bonds

Savings Bonds may be purchased in an individual name, in the name of an individual with a beneficiary (Mary Doe P.O.D. Joan Doe), in two names (but not more than two names) as joint tenants, community property, or tenants in common. The face of each bond will have the name of the party or parties and show how title is held.

.10 Vehicles

Any automobile, truck, motorcycle, or boat registered through the California Department of Motor Vehicles may be registered in a number of ways. Title may be in a single name alone. Or it may be in two names with an "or," which indicates joint tenants. Or, it may state "and" or have a slash "/" which means tenants in common. With tenants in common, each of the two parties owns one-half of the vehicle or boat. Title can also be taken in a married couple's name as community property. It is also possible to take title in a single person's name, naming a beneficiary (Mary Doe P.O.D. Joan Doe). The "Certificate of Owner-ship" to the vehicle shows how title is held. If there is a loan on the vehicle, the owner may not have the certificate of ownership, which will be held by the lender. In that case, the "Certificate of Registration," which is issued annually when the car registration is renewed, will also show title.

.11 Limited Partnerships

The limited partnership agreement will frequently show how title is held. Title may be taken in the same form as real property. If the partnership agreement does not show title, then the annual tax statement issued to the partner, the "K-1" form for federal income tax purposes, may show how title is held.

.12 Mobile Home

Registration for a mobile home is handled through the California Department of Housing and the certificate of registration for the mobile home should list the owner or owners and show how title is held.

.13 Other Assets

If there are other assets that are registered such as an airplane, a boat registered with the Coast Guard instead of the Department of Motor Vehicles, or a registered animal such as a horse or dog or any other asset, there should be papers or a certificate listing the registered owner. If the asset is registered in the name of two or more people, the document should show if title is held as joint tenants, community property, or tenant in common.

.14 Untitled Assets

Assets that do not carry a title or certificate, or form of registration are considered to be owned by the person who physically has them. Furniture, jewelry, coins, gold bullion, and other assets pass by the owner's will. These assets may be community property if the owner was married. In many cases, a married woman will leave her jewelry to her daughters if she predeceases her husband. The husband may not raise any questions, but if the jewelry is community property, the husband owns half of the jewelry.

¶203 Income Tax Cost Basis at Death

One of the more confusing questions is what the cost basis of various assets owned by the decedent at death?

"Cost basis" refers to a person's income tax basis. If the assets are sold, cost basis is used to determine the amount of the capital gain or loss. A person pays $3,000 for stock and later sells the stock for $5,000, then the cost basis is $3,000 and there is a $2,000 gain.

Cost basis is adjusted based on any additions to the assets such as an improvement. If an individual buys a home for $250,000, but adds a room that costs $25,000, the increase is cost basis by $25,000, to a total of $275,000. Conversely, reducing the value of an asset lowers the cost basis. An individual purchases rental real estate for $250,000, but under tax rules is able to depreciate the property by $100,000 over a ten-year period. The cost basis, if the property is sold, is now $150,000.

The person or people who inherit an asset obtain a new cost basis, based on the value shown on the federal estate tax return, or if there is no return, on the date of death.[13] This is an advantage for most people, since it generally increases the cost basis and therefore lowers any future capital gains tax.

For a single individual, there is a new cost basis for all of the decedent's assets. This is true even if there are insufficient assets to generate a federal estate tax return. Mary Doe dies with a home worth $250,000 and $100,000 of stock. Since the assets total less than $1,500,000, no federal estate tax is due. However, the children who inherit the estate receive a new cost basis based on the date of death value. If they sell their mother's home, they do not have to go back to the original value she paid for it, but instead use the date of death value of $250,000. If they sell it for $250,000 or less, no capital gains tax is due.

---

[13] Internal Revenue Code section 1014.

This is true even if the asset was in a living trust or in joint tenancy with a child or children. As mentioned previously, if an asset is in joint tenancy with someone other than the spouse, but was originally totally owned by the decedent, then at death it will be fully taxable for estate tax purposes. Since it is taxable, it will get a new cost basis for 100% of the asset.

If the decedent was married, there might be some confusion based on how title is held.

If the person who died owned any separate property that was solely in his or her name or was in a living trust, then all of the separate property would get a new cost basis at death.

If the assets were held by the couple in joint tenancy or held as community property, either in the couple's name or in a living trust, then the rules are different.

.01 Husband and Wife as Joint Tenants

If assets were in the name of husband and wife as joint tenants, then only one-half of each asset gets a new cost basis at death. The remaining half, which belongs to the surviving spouse, retains its original cost. A couple pays $100,000 for a home, but at the husband's death it is worth $400,000. The husband's half gets a new value of $200,000 (1/2 of the $400,000 fair market value at death). The surviving wife keeps her original cost basis of $50,000 (1/2 of the $100,000 purchase price). The adjusted cost is therefore $250,000 and if the property is sold for $400,000 there will be a $150,000 capital gains.

.02 Husband and Wife as Community Property

If the couple took title to their home as community property or hold it in a living trust as community property, then not only do the decedent's half get a new cost basis at death based on the date of death value, but the surviving spouse as well.[14] The husband's half is worth $200,000, but the surviving wife's half is also stepped up to $200,000, for a total value of $400,000. If the property is sold for $400,000, the cost basis would be $400,000 and there would be no capital gains on the sale.

It is therefore better to hold assets owned by husband and wife as community property rather than as joint tenancy where there might be a significant capital gains involved.

¶204 Safe Deposit Boxes

Safe deposit boxes cannot be held in joint tenancy. The same result may be accomplished by having another person or people as co-signers. Safe deposit boxes are not inventoried at death and have not been inventoried since the early 1980s. If there is a co-signer on the box, such as a spouse or child, that person may legally enter the safe deposit box after death and remove any or all of the contents.

---

[14] Internal Revenue Code section 1014(b)(6).

Although contents of a safe deposit box, such as bearer bonds, jewelry or coins, may not be held in joint tenancy, the co-signer of a box may enter the box after death and remove the contents. The co-signer may take assets without other family members being aware of this.

It is better to have someone as a co-signer on the safe deposit box rather than leave it in a single name alone.

¶205 Estate Taxation at Death

Although holding assets in joint tenancy avoids probate, it does not avoid taxation. The Internal Revenue Service takes the legal position that if a joint tenant dies; it is presumed that all of the assets in joint tenancy are taxable in the decedent's estate.[15]

Assets in an individual's name alone, the portion of an asset owned by the decedent as a tenant in common, one-half of all community property assets, and all joint tenancy assets are taxed when a person dies. The federal government is not concerned if probate is avoided or not, only that any estate tax which may be due is paid.

¶206 Reassessment of Real Property at Death

California's Proposition 13, which was passed in the late 1970s, provided that real property would not be reassessed other than a maximum of 2% per year unless there was a change in ownership. What constitutes a change of ownership and triggers a reassessment?

The law has carved out a number of exceptions to the reassessment. Transfers between husband and wife are exempt.[16] Also exempted are transfers between a parent or parents and children for a home no matter what the value, and other real property with a full cash value of not more than $1,000,000.[17] Real property in excess of this amount is reassessed. Step-children, in many cases, are treated as children and transfers to step-children are also exempt.[18] Transfers to son-in-laws and daughter-in-laws are exempt.[19]

A third exemption exists for transfers between grandparent and a grandchild or grandchildren if the grandchild's parents are both deceased. Again the exemption is for the family home and another $1,000,000 of real estate per deceased grandparent.[20]

In addition, real estate may be put into joint tenancy. As long as one of the original owners stays as one of the joint tenants, no reassessment is involved until the original owner dies.[21] Real estate may be transferred into a living trust that is revocable or for the benefit of a spouse or children, and no increase in taxes will occur.

---

[15] Internal Revenue Code section 2040.

[16] California Revenue and Taxation Code section 63.

[17] California Revenue and Taxation Code section 63.1(a)(1) and (2).

[18] California Revenue and Taxation Code section 63.1(c)(3)(B).

[19] California Revenue and Taxation Code section 63.1(c)(3)(C).

[20] California Revenue and Taxation Code sections 61(e), 62(f), and 65(b).

[21] California Revenue and Taxation Code sections 62(d) and 63(a).

Other than those exceptions, a death is considered a change of ownership and triggers a reassessment. Transfers of real estate to brothers or sisters, nieces or nephews, or other relatives or friends result in a reassessment. If the decedent only owned a portion of the property, and it is not exempt, only the decedent's portion is reassessed.

The county learns of this because every time a deed, affidavit, or other document is recorded which changes title, a form entitled a "preliminary change of ownership report" must also be submitted with the deed or other document to the county recorder's office.

If the preliminary change form does not indicate that the property is exempt, then the county assessor will reassess it and send out a notice of reassessment to the person or people involved. The new owners then have a limited period of time to object to the value of this reassessment. If no objections are raised, then the county tax collector sends out a supplemental tax bill for the year or years in question.

For real estate taxes, the tax year runs from July 1st to June 30th of the following year. If a person dies between these two dates, the county tax collector prorates the supplemental tax bill for the balance of the year based on the number of days of that tax year before and after the date of death. An individual dies on July 30th. Property taxes are raised from $800 per year to $4,000 per year, or a $3,200 per year increase. The bill would be prorated for the 335 days left in the tax year and the owner would receive a supplemental tax bill for the additional amount.

If a real estate deed is not recorded for several years, then the tax authorities bill for the entire period after death. There is no statute of limitations. If an estate were open for five years and no notification made, when the estate was concluded and a court order recorded changing title to the property, the county would ultimately send out supplemental tax bills for the five-year period from death.

In one case a woman died and left her home to her sister. Because of litigation, the estate was open for four years. Although the county assessor was notified, the assessor's office lost the form and did not reassess the property until after the estate was concluded. The sister received a supplemental tax bill for $6,000, which had to be paid within 30 days. The fact that the county lost the documents was not a legal excuse to delay payment or to avoid the additional taxation.

¶206

Chapter 3

PROPERTY OWNERSHIP BY HUSBAND AND WIFE

¶300 Introduction

Husband and wife may own different types of assets (community, quasi-community and separate property) based on where and how the assets were acquired. They may own the property as community property or quasi-community property. In addition, either spouse may own separate property. For estate planning purposes, it is important to analyze a couple's assets and take into account these different types of assets when planning each spouse's estate.

It is sometimes difficult to visualize the difference between how people take title to assets and how these assets are acquired. Property ownership is based on when and where assets are acquired, rather than title to these assets. A couple may hold title to assets as joint tenants, but the assets may have been acquired during marriage and may be community property in terms of their "source."

¶301 Community Property

California is one of nine states that has community property forms of ownership for husband and wife.[1] California community property is defined as assets acquired by husband and wife during the course of their marriage from the earnings of either while residents of California or another community property state or country.[2]

A couple lives in California. The husband's salary is community property. If the husband uses his salary to buy a home, stock, or other assets, these assets would be community property. The earnings on community property are also community property. If the couple purchased stock with his salary, the stock would be community property. The dividends paid on the stock would also be community property since the stock was community property. If the stock was sold and a profit made, the profit would also be community property.

Whenever one looks at an asset, the question arises as to where the funds came from to purchase the asset. If the purchase price can be traced back to community property, the asset, any earnings, and any profit upon sale, are also community property.

All earnings during marriage and all fringe benefits are considered community property. John Doe, who is married, is employed in and lives in California.

---

[1] California, Louisiana, Texas, New Mexico, Arizona, Idaho, Washington, Nevada, and Wisconsin (for assets acquired after January 1, 1986).

[2] California Probate Code section 28 and Family Code section 760.

His employer provides company paid life insurance and contributes to both a corporate pension and profit sharing plan. The life insurance and the pension and profit sharing plan would be community property because the funds that went into them were community property.

Husband and wife are the co-managers of the community property, and either spouse at death can will away his or her half of community property assets.[3] In most cases, each asset is looked at separately so that if the wife dies and wills away her half of $800,000 of community property to her children, the children do not receive $400,000 of selected assets but one-half of each individual asset, such as one-half of the home and one-half of each issue of stock

Recent changes in California law allow a couple to divide community property or quasi-community property at death based on the total value of the community or quasi-community property rather than one-half of each individual asset. To do this, the couple must have a written agreement for what is termed a "non pro rata division" of their property. This can provide greater flexibility in dividing assets at death and allow a larger amount of assets to be sheltered in a living trust.[4]

The couple can switch community property around by written agreement so that those assets then become the separate property of either spouse, or they can divide them so that each spouse takes one-half of the community property assets and they then become each spouse's separate property.

¶302 Quasi-Community Property

California is one of the few states that has a second type of property defined as quasi-community property. These assets have been acquired in a non-community property state or country during marriage and would have been community property if the couple had resided in California.[5] By moving into California, these assets become quasi-community property and at death the surviving spouse is entitled to one-half of these assets.

Husband and wife reside in New York State. Under New York State law, the husband's earnings are considered his separate property. The couple retires and moves to California. If the husband dies before the wife, at least one-half of these assets, that are now considered quasi-community property at his death, must go to the wife. If the wife dies first, she cannot dispose of any of these assets because they belong to the husband until his death.[6]

Earnings and capital gains from quasi-community property are also quasi-community property. Whoever earned the assets would be the sole manager of these assets until death.

For estate planning purposes, quasi-community property is treated similarly to community property.

---

[3] California Probate Code section 6101(b).
[4] California Probate Code section 100(b) and 101(b).

[5] California Probate Code section 66.
[6] California Probate Code section 6101(c).

¶303 Seperate Property

Either spouse may also own separate property. Separate property is defined as assets owned by the person at the time of marriage and any assets acquired after marriage by gift or inheritance. Mary Doe marries and owns $250,000 of stock and bank accounts. These assets plus their earnings and profits, if sold, are her separate property. She is the sole manager of this separate property and at her death she can will these assets to anyone she wishes.[7] She does not have to leave any of the assets at death to her husband.

After Mrs. Doe's marriage, her mother dies and Mary inherits $400,000 of stock. All of this stock is her separate property. Her father gives her $10,000 per year for several years before he dies. These gifts are also her separate property.

Many couples are concerned that when they both die and a child inherits a share of the couple's assets, the child's spouse will somehow obtain these assets. The child can leave his or her separate property to anyone he or she wishes at death, but until death it remains the child's separate property. At death the spouse has no rights to any of the separate property unless it is left to him or her, or unless the child dies without a will, in which case the spouse will inherit part of the child's separate property.

Separate property can be converted to community property but since January 1, 1985, it can only be converted by a written agreement.[8] Separate property cannot be converted by an oral agreement. Prior to 1985 oral agreements to change separate property to community property were valid and are still valid if made prior to 1985. If one spouse claims an oral agreement, then the court will have to decide if there really was such an agreement.

¶304 Written Agreement

A couple may execute a written agreement to change the character of their property. They may execute a premarital agreement before they marry. During marriage the couple may sign a community property agreement, or they may execute a post-nuptial agreement. All of these agreements are valid if properly executed.

¶305 Premarital Agreement

As the name implies, a premarital agreement is an agreement entered into by a couple before marriage. It defines what each spouse owns at the time of marriage in terms of his and her separate property and also lists any separate debts that each spouse has.[9]

In most cases, a premarital agreement recites what California law already provides if no agreement was made. In a few cases, it changes the character of the assets acquired after marriage. It may provide that the husband or wife's salary after marriage will be his or her separate property and not community property. It also can provide that in the event of divorce, the wife (or husband)

---

[7] California Probate Code section 6101(a) and Family Code section 770.

[8] California Family Code sections 850-853.

[9] California Family Code section 1612(a).

waives spousal support or receives a pre-set lump sum in lieu of monthly support.

Such an agreement is binding, and provides that both spouses have each been separately represented by an attorney, who advised that person as to his or her rights (one attorney cannot advise both parties). If an attorney represents the parties, the courts will normally not interfere with the agreement. If the wife was required to sign an agreement just before marriage giving up any rights to future community property and a separate attorney did not represent her, then the courts could invalidate the agreement.[10]

¶306 Community Property Agreement

Many couples sign a "community property agreement." This is a written document which states that all assets no matter how titled, are community property assets and will be treated as community property at death.[11] This written agreement overrides title holdings so that if a couple has assets in their names as joint tenants, or in the individual name of either spouse, the agreement changes it as if all of the assets were registered as community property.

If either spouse signs a community property agreement and has separate property, the separate property now becomes community property, unless the agreement states otherwise.

The advantage of signing a community property agreement is that it allows either spouse at death to will away his or her half of the community property. Had the assets stayed in a joint tenancy registration, the assets would have all gone to the surviving spouse as the surviving joint tenant.

Changing assets to community property also changes the income tax basis at death because both halves of the assets get a new or stepped up cost basis at the death of the first spouse. If the assets remained titled as joint tenancy assets, then only one-half of each asset would get a new cost basis at the death of the first spouse.

Many couples sign community property agreements without getting advice from their attorney, accountant, or financial advisor. Such an agreement should not be signed unless the couple understands the ramifications of such a change. Again, if either spouse had separate property and, unless the separate property is itemized in the agreement as a certain spouse's separate property, it will be converted to community property. In the case of a divorce, one-half of these assets will wind up staying with the other spouse.

¶307 Estate Planning to Determine Property Ownership

It is important for a couple to list any separate property that either owns. If either spouse had a small amount of assets at marriage, such as $10,000, this may be disregarded. Any larger amounts should be kept separate unless the couple gets professional advice and unless the spouse has advice as to whether he or she should convert the separate property to community property.

---

[10] California Family Code section 1615(c).   [11] California Family Code section 1500.

If all of the couple's assets are community property and/or quasi-community property then generally no change needs to be undertaken, other than to make everything community property.

If a couple decides to change assets so that everything is community property, it can be handled in one of several ways. Assets can be changed so that the title is in the couples name as "community property." Assets may also be transferred into a living trust with a schedule that lists the assets transferred as "community property." Or the couple may execute a community property agreement stating that everything they own is community property.

Chapter 4

INCAPACITY

¶400 Introduction

With people living longer, it is important to discuss what happens if a person becomes incapacitated. What if the person has a stroke and is unable to sign documents, speak, or make medical care decisions?

What if a person is unable to care for themselves such as feeding themselves, dressing and handling the normal affairs of everyday life? Can the person handle his or her financial affairs? Is the person subject to undue influence or fraud by relatives or "friends?"

Most people tend to ignore these matters as long as the person is alert and able to fend for him or herself. But sometimes children find an aged parent who is throwing away checks and other legal documents. Someone may discover that a relative is giving funds to people whom phone saying that the relative has won a contest or new car and requests $5,000 or $10,000. Or the relative gets a telephone call and it is later discovered that she has purchased $5,000 worth of vitamins using her credit card. Maybe the relative puts important papers in the refrigerator or under the bed or in some other hidden place. Or the widowed father in his 80s is giving away large amounts of money to his new, 23-year-old, girlfriend.

Alzheimer's or other diseases can be devastating for a spouse or children who are attempting to cope with and help the afflicted spouse or parent.

In addition to all of the emotional problems that are involved, there are many legal questions that arise and must be addressed. If the individual lacks the capacity to understand what he or she is doing, then he or she cannot sign a living trust agreement, will, power of attorney, or other document. Documents must be signed before the person becomes incapacitated.

A number of legal options are available if planning has been done. The California Legislature also has set up a complex procedure if no planning has been done.

¶401 Joint Tenancy

It is possible to hold virtually any asset in joint tenancy. Mary Doe places her home, securities, and bank accounts all in joint tenancy with her two children. She later has a stroke and is totally incapacitated. What can the children do now in terms of managing her assets?

If bank or savings association accounts are in joint tenancy, normally any one of the joint tenants can deposit checks, even without the check being endorsed, and any one of them can write checks or make withdrawals from the account. Dividend and interest checks which are payable to Mary Doe can still be deposited. Checks can be written for doctor and other bills. However, stock and real estate, which is in joint tenancy, requires all of the joint tenants'signatures before taking any action. If the children wish to sell a portion of the stock, they must get their mom to sign the stock certificates or have a power of attorney from her.

If any legal matters have to be undertaken, such as signing income tax returns or other legal documents, the children will be unable to do so without a durable power of attorney or a conservatorship. Joint tenancy works well for bank and savings association accounts, vehicles, and U.S. Savings Bonds since any one of the joint tenants can take action. This does not work for securities, mutual funds, or real estate, because all of the joint tenants must sign before any action can be taken.

¶402 Conservatorship

California law provides a court procedure if a person becomes so incapacitated that the person is unable to feed or cloth themselves, or look after their financial affairs.[1] This procedure is a complex, costly and time consuming process. Because the person is alive, the legislature has built in a number of safeguards to protect the person's rights.

Many times clients have their minister or physician recommend that they act as "conservator" for a relative. In many cases, the person is handling the relative's affairs under a durable power of attorney without difficulty. It is recommended that one not undertake a conservatorship unless it is absolutely necessary, and there are no other alternatives available.

A conservatorship comprises two areas; conservator of the person and conservator of the estate. A conservator of the person is needed when the individual is unable to take care of his or her basic needs such as feeding or clothing themselves. A conservator of the estate is needed if the person is unable to manage his or her assets or resist fraud or undue influence. Normally, the nearest relative, such as a spouse or child, has the first right to be conservator. A person can also sign a document entitled "nomination of conservator" while he or she is still able, and nominate someone if a conservator is later required, and the person does not wish the nearest relative to serve.

A bank may be the conservator of the estate if the assets subject to a conservatorship are large enough in value, frequently $500,000 to $1,500,000 minimum. The conservator of the estate receives an annual fee (subject to court approval), annually, based on the value of the conservatorship assets. A bank that is handling an estate of $2,300,000, receives an annual fee of approximately $23,000.

Since an attorney is involved, there are legal fees for establishing the conservatorship and legal fees for the regular accounting required by the court. The costs can amount to $2,000 to $5,000 to establish the conservatorship and $2,000 to $10,000 per year for the legal work involved.

[1] California Probate Code sections 1800-1835.

¶402

There are also court filing fees, investigator fees, appraisal fees, and numerous other legal costs.

A conservatorship is a legal action filed in the county superior court where the person (called a "conservatee") resides. The petition is set for hearing by the court approximately 60 days after it is filed. The proposed conservatee must either appear in court or have a physician declare that he or she is physically or mentally unable to appear in court. If the person is unable to appear in court, the court will appoint an investigator to interview the proposed conservatee and report back to the court.

In addition, a citation must be personally served on the individual and certain relatives, such as children, parents, brothers, and sisters, must be given notice of the court hearing. If the proposed conservatee indicates that he or she objects to the conservatorship, the court must appoint an attorney to represent the person.

Once the conservator is appointed, an inventory must be filed with the court listing the assets and their current value with the court. An accounting of all funds received and disbursed must be filed with the court one year after the initial appointment and every two years thereafter.

The conservatorship continues until the person regains his or her capacity to manage their assets or until his or her death. Younger people may recover, but conservatorships for older people frequently continue until death, when a probate is generally necessary.

Because of the costs and cumbersome nature, conservatorships should be undertaken only as the last resort. Unfortunately, if the proposed conservatee had done no planning, such as establishing a living trust or executing a general durable power of attorney, a conservatorship proceeding may be required.

¶403 Durable Power of Attorney

One alternative to a conservatorship is for the person, while legally able, to execute a "durable power of attorney." A power of attorney is a document signed by the person and notarized, which gives someone the right to legally act as agent for that person. California has enacted legislation that governs the execution of durable powers of attorney.[2]

The person who gives a power of attorney is the "principal." The person who is given the power of attorney is the "agent." In naming an agent, one can name several people together. If an individual names two or more persons, one should indicate whether they must act together, "jointly," or whether any of the parties may act on ones behalf alone,"severally."[3] An individual may also name several people in order to handle affairs upon incapacity. A wife could be named as the primary agent, and if she is deceased or unable to act, a child may then serve.[4]

---

[2] California Probate Code sections 4000-4310.
[3] California Probate Code section 4202.

[4] California Probate Code section 4203.

The power of attorney should also indicate that it continues if the principal becomes incapacitated.[5] The fact that it continues makes it a "durable" power of attorney. If such a statement is not in the power of attorney, then it terminates upon the principal's incapacity. A power of attorney, whether durable or not, always terminates when the principal dies.

The power of attorney can be very broad and can give the agent or agents power to sign for the principal, sell assets, make gifts, among other things. It is possible for the courts to review the actions taken by an agent under a power of attorney. This protects the principal to some degree, but it also can impose a burden on the agent, who must later account for all of his actions and decisions.

Most powers of attorney are "general" powers of attorney. They are effective immediately, give the agent very broad authority and continue until revoked by the principal or until the principal's death. The power of attorney can be revoked and canceled by the principal at any time.

A few powers of attorney are "limited" powers of attorney.[6] These either continue for a short period of time, such as when the principal is out of the country on a long trip for six to eight months. Or the power of attorney may be for a specific asset. A principal and his brother jointly own the family home after their parents' death. The brother is attempting to sell the home that is in another state. Rather than have all of the legal documents signed by both brothers, one brother may give the other brother a limited power of attorney which allows him to sign all documents with regard to the sale of the home, but it does not extend to other assets.

Some people don't wish to give someone a broad power to handle their assets. But they do want the power of attorney to take effect only if they become incapacitated. For these people a "springing" power of attorney may be appropriate. A springing power of attorney only becomes effective upon certain event, such as when two doctors certify, in writing, that the principal is incapacitated and unable to manage his or her assets.[7] With the power of attorney and the doctor's written certification, the agent can then act.

The disadvantage of a "springing" power of attorney is that the organization the agent is dealing with, such as the bank or brokerage firm, may decline to accept the document because the organization is unsure if the doctors' certification is acceptable. On occasion, when an agent has presented the springing power of attorney to a brokerage firm, the firm has declined to accept and told the agent to use a conservatorship proceeding because the brokerage firm thought it would be better.

Banks and savings associations often have their own form of power of attorney for accounts at the institution. Many insist that their forms be used and will refuse to accept any other power of attorney. The choice is to use their form or get involved in a lengthy and costly lawsuit with the financial organization.

[5] California Probate Code section 4124.
[6] California Probate Code section 4262.
[7] California Probate Code section 4129.

¶403

Many title companies will not accept a power of attorney if the power of attorney is too old, or "stale." A power of attorney that is more than six months old may not be acceptable.

While California law relieves any person or organization receiving a power of attorney from any liability in connection with the power of attorney, despite the fact that it is valid, everyone still does not always accept it.

California has enacted legislation that creates a uniform statutory form power of attorney. If the law is followed, a simple form can be used which is filled in, signed, and notarized. This form can be obtained from many stationery stores or health care organizations.[8]

¶404 Living Trust

Many people use a living trust in connection with the person's estate plan. Under the living trust (discussed in Chapter 10), a trustee is appointed to manage and administer the trust. Generally, the creator of the trust acts as his or her own trustee. Upon that person's incapacity, death, or resignation, another trustee takes over the management of the trust. Incapacity is usually defined as a case in which two doctors have examined the person and state in writing that, in their opinion, the person is not able to manage his or her financial affairs. No court procedure is required.

Mary Doe establishes a living trust with herself as the initial trustee. She transfers all of the assets she owns to the trust. She becomes incapacitated and under the trust agreement her daughter is named as the successor trustee. With the two doctors'certification, the daughter legally takes over the management of all of the trust assets.

A living trust avoids probate and also avoids problems caused by the trustee's incapacity. For the trust to be effective, the person must have signed the living trust, transferred assets to the trust, and have provision in the trust to cover incapacity.

¶405 Durable Power of Attorney for Health Care

A second type of power of attorney is available in California. This is called a durable power of attorney for health care. Over the years, the California legislature has wrestled with the problem of how to handle a situation where a person is unable to make decisions regarding their medical care and treatment. It was decided to use a legal document that appoints someone to make these decisions if the person is unable to make them.[9]

This document is called a "durable power of attorney for health care." Over the years, it has been revised on several occasions. Since 1992, if a person signs this form, it is good indefinitely, unless revoked. Prior to 1992, it was only good for a seven-year period and had to be renewed at the end of the seven-year period.

---

[8] California Probate Code sections 4400-4465.   [9] California Probate Code sections 4600-4805.

There are a number of different types of forms available. One is printed in the California Probate Code.[10] Another has been put together and sold by the California Medical Association. Many attorneys devise their own form and use it for their clients. Any of the forms can be used. It is also possible to devise one's own form and customize it for the person signing it.

The form allows the principal to name only one agent at a time to make medical decisions. If a parent has three children, the three children can not be named jointly. They can be named in some order, but only one at a time can act. The power of attorney only comes into play if, in the doctor's opinion, the principal is not able to make medical decisions.

The agent, acting under this document, has the legal authority to examine the principal's medical records, consent to or withhold consent to medical treatment, consent to having the principal taken off of a life support system (if in the doctor's opinion the principal would not likely live if taken off the machine), and at death, the agent can also consent to donation of body organs for transplant purposes and arrange for the funeral and burial or cremation. The agent may also request an autopsy if the agent wishes one.[11]

All of the above are subject to the principal's written directions. These can be customized on the form. The form either requires two witnesses to the principal's signature, or it may alternatively be notarized. None of the agents may be the owners or managers of a convalescent hospital, and the agent may not be a doctor unless the doctor is related to the principal by blood or marriage. If the principal is a patient in a convalescent hospital, there also must be a witness who is a state certified ombudsman for the facility. This ombudsman must discuss the document with the principal and must be a witness to it before it is valid.[12]

¶406 Living Will

The term "living will" refers to a document in which a person requests that he or she be allowed to die a natural death and not be kept alive by artificial means or a life support system. California formerly had a document which was called a "directive to physician." This was very similar to a living will, but this form was abolished by the California Legislature in 1992.

Many forms entitled "living will" are sold to the public by various organizations. None of these forms has any legal basis. Although physicians and hospitals may accept the form as the patient's intent, in the event that they fail to accept it, there is no legal authority for forcing them to do so.

¶407 Request to Forgo Resuscitative Measures

When someone dials 911 for emergency medical assistance or is taken to a hospital emergency room, the patient is treated and the concern is to keep the person alive and stabilized until a doctor can determine treatment. Many people who are terminally ill do not wish "heroic measures" to be undertaken to keep them alive in such a situation.

[10] California Probate Code sections 4701.
[11] California Probate Code section 4683
[12] California Probate Code section 4673.

California law allows a person and his or her doctor to execute a form entitled "Request to forgo resuscitative measures." This is used when a person is diagnosed as being terminally ill and desires to die naturally without any resuscitative measures being taken to keep the person alive. The form can be obtained from the person's attending physician and then must be signed by the individual or his or her healthcare decision maker and by the physician.[13]

¶408 Donation of Body Organs

The donation of body organs at death has become more of a concern in recent years because of the need for these organs and the ability of medical science to "transplant" these organs to people who need them. How are these organs obtained?

Approval may be obtained from the nearest relatives at death if the decedent has not indicated in writing that he did not wish organs donated. Alternatively, the person may fill out a donor card with the Department of Motor Vehicles, which is placed with his driver's license, list such permission in his will, have separate written instructions, or the consent may be made by an agent under a durable power of attorney for health care after death.[14]

¶409 Gift of Body to Medical Science

Occasionally, a person wishes to donate his or her body to medical science upon death. A "State Curator" has the power to accept such a body for the medical schools in this state. No guarantee is made and occasionally there are more bodies than needed so the body is rejected.

If the body is accepted, all costs of transportation must be borne by the family or relatives. In one instance, a person left his body to science, and it was accepted. His children were startled to discover a bill for $350 for transporting the body to a medical center in San Francisco.

¶410 Medi-Cal/Medicaid

When a person has to enter a convalescent hospital, there is almost always a concern as to the cost and the depletion of the individual's cash and assets. With costs running $6,000 or more per month, the question arises as to whether the state or federal government will pay a portion or all of these costs. The answer generally is "No."

People who are covered by Medicare and private or supplemental medical insurance may have a portion of the convalescent hospital bills paid in some cases. If a person goes into a hospital for medical treatment and is then transferred to a convalescent hospital for recuperation or medical care, the costs are partially paid, but only for a limited period of time. 90 days is usually the limit and the costs are rarely paid by an insurance carrier in full. If a person has a hip replacement and spends 60 days recuperating in a convalescent hospital, insurance may pay a portion of the cost.

---

[13] California Probate Code section 4780-4786.

[14] California Health and Safety Code sections 7150-7156.

If, however, the person suffers from Alzheimer's disease and needs custodial care, then insurance will not pay for any of the costs. The cost will have to be borne by the individual or his relatives.

It is possible to purchase special convalescent hospital insurance which will pay these costs, but the policy must be purchased before the individual has a condition which would disqualify him. Also, many policies will not accept an applicant after age 80, if the policy is taken out before that time though, it will be good after the person attains age 80. A number of policies are written by different insurance companies and if a person investigates these policies, they should be aware of the maximum benefits payable under the policy (frequently a five year or shorter limit), the maximum monthly amount payable, and the elimination period before the policy starts to pay after the person goes into a convalescent hospital (frequently 90 to 180 days).

Many people, upon learning that their mother is going into a convalescent hospital and looking at costs of over $70,000 per year, attempt to figure out some way to prevent these costs from exhausting their mom's estate, leaving no inheritance at death for her children.

All of the states in the United States have a joint federal/state funded medical assistance program to pay for people who do not have assets or funds to pay for their medical costs. These programs are referred to as Medicaid programs in all states except California. In California the program is called Medi-Cal.

To be eligible for assistance, an applicant may have a home, car, furniture, and a few other personal assets. His or her cash, other assets such as real estate (other than his or her home), and securities cannot exceed approximately $2,000. If the person has more than that amount, he or she must spend down to this minimum before applying for Medi-Cal assistance. If the person is married, the spouse may not have assets other than the home of more than approximately $85,000.

The application won't work if an applicant decides to give away his or her assets and apply for assistance. The government generally considers any gifts made within 36 months of application as also being owned by the applicant.[15] In some cases, gifts made over 36 months before application are also counted. In addition, if the person is not married and owns a home, the government agency may require that the home be sold six months after leaving the home and the person then becomes ineligible for Medi-Cal because of the cash proceeds from the sale.

If the home is not sold or if there is a surviving spouse, California places a lien on the home to obtain reimbursement for money spent when the home is later sold. There is also a provision that when a person dies, anyone who inherits, whether by a probate proceeding, joint tenancy, or living trust, must advise the California Department of Health Services so that they may file an appropriate claim and obtain full reimbursement for money previously spent.[16]

---

[15] 42 United States Code 1396p(c)(1)(B)(i).   [16] California Probate Code section 9202.

¶410

Planners handle many estates where the State has filed a claim and obtained reimbursement. In most of these cases, the decedent had a home that was not sold during lifetime. After death, the home went through a probate procedure and the State filed a creditor's claim and obtained full reimbursement after the home was sold. In one case the amount was over $78,000.

There are some things that can be done to reduce the amount that the government receives by way of reimbursement at death. Any person who faces or has a relative facing this situation should consult an attorney who specializes in elder care law and who is well versed in this area of laws.

¶411 Conclusion

Estate planning involves not just the planning of the disposition of assets at death, but also the management of assets if the person becomes incapacitated. Most people should have a durable power of attorney and a durable power of attorney for health care. This is true even if the individual has a will and living trust.

In addition, the question of how possible future convalescent hospital bills will be paid needs to be answered.

Chapter 5

WILLS AND INTESTATE SUCCESSION

¶500 Introduction

A will is the cornerstone of any estate plan. If one does not make a will before they die, one dies "intestate" and the State of California makes the will. The assets then go to nearest relatives, whether wanted or not.

Many people think that a will controls all of the person's assets at death. This isn't true. A will does not control assets that are in joint tenancy, life insurance where a beneficiary has been named, and certain other types of assets.

¶501 What a Will Is

A will is a legal document executed in accordance with state law, which disposes of a person's assets at death. The will must be valid in the state in which the decedent lived at the time of death.

Any person 18 years of age or older, who is competent, may make a will.[1] Competency is a legal term, but it means that the maker of the will (called the "testator") understands that the document they are signing is their will and that they know who their nearest relatives are and what assets they own.[2]

Even if a person is suffering from a mental disorder, unless the mental disorder causes an individual to leave their property in an unusual way, the will is still valid.[3] A will is presumed valid.

If anyone contests the will after death, the contestant must prove that there was undue influence, fraud, or that the testator lacked mental capacity to make a will.[4]

California recognizes two types of wills. A witnessed will is a will signed by the testator in the presence of two witnesses who then sign as witnesses to the will.[5] A holographic or handwritten will is a will in which all of the material portions are in the testator's handwriting (not typed or computer generated); it is signed by the testator, and dated. If it is not dated and there are no other wills, then the lack of a date will not make it invalid. No witnesses are required.[6] Many people handwrite their own wills.

California also has two types of statutory wills.[7] These are fixed, preprinted will forms with two or more witnesses. California law also recognizes other types of wills. A will under the Uniform International Wills Act is valid, as is a will which was valid where it was executed, valid where the testator resided at the

---

[1] California Probate Code section 6100.
[2] California Probate Code section 6100.5.
[3] California Probate Code section 6100(a)(2).
[4] California Probate Code section 6104.
[5] California Probate Code section 6110.
[6] California Probate Code section 6111.
[7] California Probate Code section 6200-6243.

time of execution of the will, or valid where the testator lived or was a national.[8] Wills executed in other states or countries are nearly always valid in California.

An oral will is not valid, nor is a video taped will, if there is no separate written will.

¶502 Who May Inherit

Under California law one may leave assets to anyone they wish.[9] Many countries and states have restrictions, and a portion of the testator's assets must go to the spouse, children or other relatives. That is not true in California. A person may disinherit his spouse, children, grandchildren and other relatives and leave assets to anyone that he or she wishes.

A person may leave their assets to any individual; a corporation, an unincorporated association, society, or lodge; a city, county or government agency; the State of California or any other state; the federal government or any political subdivision; and any foreign government. One cannot leave assets directly to an animal. If this is done, the court will convert this to a trust to take care of the animal until its death.[10]

¶503 Assets Controlled By a Will

While not all assets are covered by a will, a person may will away the following assets.[11]

1. All separate property of a married person, which is in his or her name alone. Separate property refers to what the decedent owned before marriage and any assets acquired during marriage by gift or an inheritance.

2. If the decedent is single, all assets in his or her name alone.

3. One-half of each asset that is titled in the husband and wife's names as community property.

4. The portion that the decedent owned and which was registered with others as tenants in common.

5. Any assets that are not registered but were owned by the decedent, such as furniture, jewelry, coins, etc.

¶504 Assets Not Controlled By a Will

One cannot control certain assets by a will since these assets are controlled by other documents or by law. These include:

1. Assets that are registered in joint tenancy with another person or persons. By law, these assets automatically go to the survivor or survivors.

2. Assets that are subject to a beneficiary designation such as life insurance, annuities, IRA accounts and pension and profit-sharing plans. The beneficiary designation supersedes the will.

3. Assets that are held in a living trust. The trust agreement or declaration states what happens to these assets at death.

---

[8] California Probate Code section 6113.
[9] California Probate Code section 6102.
[10] California Probate Code section 15212.
[11] California Probate Code section 6101.

4. Assets in the decedent's name as "trustee for" someone. The person or people named as beneficiary will receive these assets at death.

5. Any assets in the decedent's name which are P.O.D. (payable on death) to another. The named beneficiary will receive the assets.

6. Any securities in the decedent's name which are T. O. D. (transfer of death) to another. The named beneficiary will receive the assets.

¶505 Intestate Succession

If a person dies intestate (without a will) then the state where the decedent resides makes the rules as to who inherits the decedent's property.[12] The only exception is with regard to real property. The laws of the state where the real property is located control real estate.

If John Doe, who is a California resident, dies without a will, then California rules of intestate succession apply as to his bank accounts, securities, real estate in California and other assets. If he also owns real property in Oregon, the rules of intestate succession for the State of Oregon will apply to the real estate in that state.

The term, "issue by right of representation" is frequently used. This means that if someone is deceased, his or her share passes to his or her "issue," or descendants. John Doe dies without a will but leaves three living children and no deceased children. Each of his children would receive one-third of his estate. If he had two living children and one deceased child who in turn had two children, then one-third of his estate would go to each of his two living children and one-third would pass to the children of the deceased child. These two grandchildren would each receive one-sixth.

This concept also applies to other relatives such as brothers, sisters and cousins. John Doe dies without any close relatives but with three living brothers and two deceased brothers who had children. His estate would be divided into five parts with each living brother getting one-fifth and one-fifth being divided among the children of each deceased brother, with the children of each deceased brother receiving equal amounts.

.01 Intestate Succession - Single Person

If the decedent was unmarried at the time of death, his or her assets go to the following people in order:[13]

1. Children.

2. Grandchildren.

3. Great grandchildren.

4. Parents equally, or to the surviving parent if one parent is deceased.

5. Brothers and sisters equally (half brothers and sisters are considered the same as full brothers and sisters) with provision that if any of the brothers and sisters are deceased, a share passes to the deceased brother's or sister's children.

6. Living grandparents equally.

---

[12] California Probate Code section 6400.   [13] California Probate Code section 6402.

7. The descendants of grandparents, such as aunts, uncles and cousins.

8. The descendants of a predeceased spouse (step-children).

9. Parent or parents of a predeceased spouse.

10. Descendants of the parents of a predeceased spouse, such as brother-in-law or sister-in-law or that person's children.

11. The next of kin or nearest blood relative.

12. The next of kin or nearest relative of a predeceased spouse.

13. If none of the above, then to the State of California.

In addition, there is a special law that if a single person dies without living children, grandchildren or great-grandchildren and previously inherited from a spouse, what was previously inherited goes back to the deceased spouse's relatives.[14]

John Doe dies with a home in joint tenancy with his wife, Mary Doe. Mary Doe dies within 15 years of her husband without a will. She has no children or grandchildren. Her nearest relatives are her brothers and sisters. Since she has no close relatives, what she has inherited from her husband goes back to his nearest relatives. In this example, one-half of the home would pass to the deceased husband's nearest relatives.

The right of inheritance for relatives of a predeceased spouse only occurs when there is real property involved and both spouses die within a 15 year period,[15] or when there is personal property (all assets other than real property) and the spouses both die within a five year period.[16]

.02 Definition of "Child"

There are a number of special provisions relating to the definition of "child" or "children."

A stepchild or foster child may, in some cases, inherit from a stepparent or foster parent. This occurs when the relationship of a stepchild or foster child started when the child was under 18 years of age and continued throughout the parties'lifetimes. It is also necessary that it be established by clear and convincing evidence that the stepparent or foster parent would have adopted the child but for some legal prohibition, such as the natural parent refusing to allow a stepparent to adopt the child.[17]

There are no requirements that the parents of a child be married at the time of birth.[18] "Illegitimate" children have the same rights of inheritance as do legitimately born children. As long as paternity is clear, the child may inherit from the father even though the father was never married to the mother.

An adopted child normally inherits from the adopted parents and not from the natural parent or parents. However, an adopted child may still inherit from the natural parent after an adoption (in addition to inheriting from the adopted parent) if the natural parent and the child lived together as parent or child and

---

[14] California Probate Code section 6402.5.

[15] California Probate Code section 6402.5(a).

[16] California Probate Code section 6402.5(b).

[17] California Probate Code section 6454.

[18] California Probate Code section 6452.

the adoption was by the spouse of either natural parent or after the death of either of the natural parents.[19]

.03 Intestate Succession - Married Person

The rules as to who inherits for a person who is married are quite different.

The rights of inheritance vary depending upon whether the assets are community property, quasi-community property, or the deceased person's separate property. If Jane Doe, who is married, dies and has $250,000 of stock in her name alone, it is first necessary to determine how this stock has been acquired. Has it been acquired during marriage while living in California or another community property state, or acquired in a non-community property state?

If the assets are community property or quasi-community property, then all of the assets pass to the surviving spouse. None of the assets pass to other relatives.[20]

If Jane Doe owned stock at the time she was married, or the stock was later acquired during marriage by gift or by inheritance, then the stock would be her separate property. Separate property goes partially to the surviving spouse and partially to other relatives, as follows:[21]

If there is only one child, or children of a deceased child, 1/2 goes to the child or issue of the deceased child and 1/2 goes to the surviving spouse or domestic partner.

If there are two or more children, 2/3 goes to the children equally and 1/3 goes to the surviving spouse or domestic partner.

If there are no children or grandchildren, 1/2 goes to the decedent's parents equally, or to the surviving parent if one is deceased, and 1/2 goes to the surviving spouse or domestic partner.

If there are no children, grandchildren or parents of the decedent, then 1/2 goes to the decedent's brothers and sisters equally, and 1/2 goes to the surviving spouse or domestic partner. If any of the brothers and sisters are deceased and have children, the deceased sibling's children would take the deceased sibling's share. Half-brothers and half-sisters take the same amount as full brothers and sisters.

Finally, if the decedent left no children, grandchildren, parents, brothers and sisters, or nieces and nephews, then all of the separate property passes to the surviving spouse or domestic partner.

.04 Domestic Partner

California law was changed effective January 1, 2003, to recognize the legal rights of a domestic partner. A "domestic partner" is defined as 1) a person of the same sex, or 2) a person of the opposite sex, if either partner is over age 62 and eligible for old-age insurance benefits under social security law. The partners must have registered a Declaration of Domestic Partnership with the California Secretary of State and not revoked this declaration prior to death.

---

[19] California Probate Code section 6453.

[20] California Probate Code sections 6401(a) and (b).

[21] California Probate Code section 6401(c).

With regard to intestate succession, the surviving domestic partner inherits the same as would a spouse where the decedent owned separate property. Thus, depending on the category of other relatives, the domestic partner inherits one-third, one-half, or all of the deceased domestic partner's assets. California Probate Code sections 37 and 6401(c) as well as Family Code section 297 cover this.

¶506 Competency to Make a Will

To make a will a person must be 18 years of age or older and must be "competent." Competency means that the person knows who his or her nearest relatives are and generally what the person owns in terms of his or her assets.[22] The testator must understand that the document he or she is signing is his or her will.

Objections can be raised to a will, after death, because of fraud (the person didn't know what he or she was signing), undue influence (someone convinced the person to leave the assets to them), or lack of capacity to make a will. A person is presumed competent to make a will, and if someone objects to the will, the objector must prove that the testator was not competent when the will was signed.

A will can be revoked or cancelled a number of different ways.[23] A person can make a new will to specifically cancels the old will. It can be torn up, destroyed or obliterated by the testator or at the testator's discretion. If there are several duplicate wills signed by the testator and any one of them is revoked, this cancels all of the copies.

Divorce revokes all provisions in the will regarding the former spouse upon the final dissolution of the marriage. The former spouse cannot inherit or act as executor, guardian or trustee.[24]

If a person dies and he or she had possession of the will and the will cannot be located, the presumption is that the decedent revoked and voluntarily destroyed the will before death.[25] Although this can be refuted, the presumption is that the person wanted it destroyed.

¶507 Joint and Mutual Wills

Very occasionally, a husband and wife will sign one document that is their joint will. Because of potential problems this is not recommended. Separate but similar wills, sometimes referred to as "mirror" wills should be signed.

A joint and mutual will can be construed as a contract to make a will. This means that the surviving spouse must leave the first spouse's assets to whoever is stated in the will. For example, the husband leaves his share of the couple's assets to his wife with the understanding that these assets will go to his brother at his wife's death. If the wife changes the will after her husband dies, then the husband's brother may sue to obtain his inheritance.

If people want to provide for someone such as a spouse and then leave the assets at the spouse's death to other people, a trust should be used instead of a will.

---

[22] California Probate Code section 6100.5(a)(1).   [24] California Probate Code section 6122.
[23] California Probate Code section 6120.   [25] California Probate Code section 6124.

¶508 Bequests in a Will

When drafting a will there are a number of ways to handle leaving an asset or assets to someone.[26]

A *specific* bequest names a specific asset such as 100 shares of XYZ stock or a specific parcel of real property. If the decedent did not own the asset at death, then the recipient does not get anything else as a substitute.

A *general* bequest is one of cash. If $25,000 is given to ones sister, she gets this amount. If one has sufficient assets but not enough cash to pay the bequest, then assets have to be sold to raise the funds.

A *demonstrative* bequest is one paid out of a specific fund. If $25,000 is given to my sister but direct that it be paid out of ones Bank of America checking account, the funds must come specifically out of that account if there is enough money. If there are insufficient funds in the account, she gets the balance of the account and not the full amount.

A *general pecuniary devise* is a dollar amount which is paid in assets, valued as of the date of distribution. If specified, the $25,000 bequest to a sister can be paid to her in stock, it is valued at the date that the stock is transferred to her.

An *annuity* is an amount of money paid monthly, quarterly, annually, or over some specific period of time.

A *residuary* devise is a bequest of what is left over after everything else is paid. The residue of the estate is what is left after expenses, taxes, costs, and all of the other devises.

Unless a person specifies, all costs, debts and expenses are paid out of the residue of an estate. Unless specified, all estate taxes are paid by each party, out of what he or she inherits. If a sister receives $25,000, and her share of the estate taxes is 15% or $3,750, she will only receive $21,250 when the estate is closed.

¶509 Subjects and People Covered by a Will

A will needs to do a number of things. A will should specifically revoke all prior wills and codicils that the testator has made. California has the unusual rule that unless you specifically revoke prior wills and codicils, they are still valid.[27] If you leave a specific cash bequest to someone and then make a new will that does not revoke the former will or cancel the cash bequest, the cash bequest under the prior will is still valid.

Certain people should be mentioned in a will. The will should specifically mention a spouse, living children, and children of a deceased child.

If a person marries after making a will or have a child or children after the will is signed, the parties are considered "forgotten" and have a right to inherit what that person would receive by intestate succession if the testator died without a will.[28] John Doe marries but does not change his will to mention his wife. At his death, she is considered a "pretermitted" heir and can claim 1/3 to

---

[26] California Probate Code section 21117.
[27] California Probate Code section 6120.
[28] California Probate Code section 6560.

1/2 of his separate property, depending upon his relatives. It is very important to make a new will or codicil mentioning the spouse.

An individual does not have to leave $1 or any amount to someone, but should mention the person in the will. Many people want to put a clause in the person's will that if someone contests the will, he is left $1. This is unnecessary. If the will is contested and is held invalid, the $1 clause is cancelled and the person inherits. If he contests and loses, they get nothing.

One alternative to try to prevent a person from contesting a will is to provide that he or she is left an amount, such as $10,000, and if he or she contests the will, they forfeit the inheritance if they lose the will contest. The person then has to make a choice about taking the money or rolling the dice for all or nothing in a will contest.

If a beneficiary dies before a testator, then who inherits the bequest left to the deceased person? The will should provide for this possibility. If a person leaves $10,000 to their brother, what happens to this amount if the brother dies before they do? It should specify that it goes to the brother's children equally or it is cancelled and goes back in with the residue of the estate. If nothing is written in the will and the beneficiary is related to the testator, then the bequest goes to the beneficiary's children. If the beneficiary is not related, the bequest lapses and goes with the residue of the estate.

If one does not specify what happens to the bequest and the brother dies ahead of the testator, the $10,000 goes to his children. If the beneficiary is a brother-in-law and the testator did not specify what happens to the bequest, then the $10,000 is cancelled and put in with the residue of the estate.

¶510 Survival Period

It is possible to put a survival period in a will so that a beneficiary does not inherit unless he or she outlives the survival period. A survival period is frequently put in the will so that if two parties, such as husband and wife, die within a very short period, the assets will not go to different parties than expected. A husband wishes to leave his estate to his wife but if she dies one day after he does, he doesn't want his assets to go to the wife's distant relatives.

A survival period should not exceed six months. Normally, a 30-day survival period will be sufficient.

Under intestate law, any heir must survive for 120 hours (5 days) before heirship is determined.[29] If an heir dies within the 120 hour period, he or she does not inherit. If an individual dies without a will and his or her brother who inherits dies three days later, the brother is treated as if he died ahead of the individual and does not inherit.

¶511 Exoneration-Ademption-Advancement

"Exoneration" means that if real property is left to someone, any loan or debt on the real property is paid in full before the beneficiary receives the property, under California law, there is no exoneration.[30] This means that if you inherit a $300,000 piece of property with a $100,000 loan against the property, the

---

[29] California Probate Code section 6403.   [30] California Probate Code section 21131.

loan is not paid off, but you receive the property subject to the loan. The only exception is if the decedent's will specifically directs that the loan be paid after death from the other assets of the estate.

"Ademption" means that the asset left by the will does not exist at death.[31] John Doe leaves 100 shares of XYZ stock to a cousin. Prior to death, he sells all of the XYZ stock. What does his cousin receive at death? In most cases, nothing is received. There are some exceptions, such as when a company has merged with another company prior to the decedent's death or when real estate is sold but a note for part of the sales price is taken back by the seller. In these cases, the person receives the merged stock or the note for the balance of the purchase price (but not any other money received before death). If a person leaves 100 shares of stock to their grandson and the stock splits 2 for 1 prior to ones death, the grandson will then receive the 200 shares of stock.

"Advancement" is where the decedent satisfied the bequest by giving it to the person prior to death. John Doe leaves $10,000 to his older sister. His sister needed the money before he died, so he gave her $10,000 prior to his death.

An advancement is only deducted from the beneficiary's share if the decedent's will provided for such deduction, if at the time of the gift the decedent left a written statement that it was to be treated as an advancement and deducted, or if the beneficiary who received the bequest stated in writing that it was treated as an advancement.[32]

If a person wants to advance a cash bequest but does not want it also paid under the will, he should either make a codicil to the will canceling the bequest or leave a written statement that he has advanced the funds and does not want it paid under the will.

¶512 Executor-Trustee-Guardian

A person's will should name an executor. An *executor* is a person, persons or bank appointed by the court to carry out all of the duties required when someone dies. The executor must collect assets subject to probate, have the assets valued, sell whatever is necessary, pay all of the bills and debts, pay all required taxes, and distribute the assets in accordance with the will.

Chapter 6 covers the probate procedure, which is rather involved. An executor does not have to live in California or even in the United States. The executor should have enough available time to take care of these duties. Anyone 18 years of age or older who has not been convicted of theft or a related offense may serve as an executor.[33] It is also possible to name a California bank or trust company as executor, although many financial institutions will not serve if the probate estate is under $500,000.

A person can name several parties jointly as co-executors, although they must work together and jointly sign all documents and checks. Or a person may name several people in the order to serve. A husband may name his wife as executor and then his three children jointly as co-executors if the wife cannot serve. Or, he may name his son as sole executor if the wife cannot serve.

---

[31] California Probate Code section 21132(a).   [33] California Probate Code section 8402.
[32] California Probate Code section 21135.

If there is no probate because all of the decedent's assets were in joint tenancy or in a living trust, then there is no executor. An executor acts only after appointment by the court and where there is a probate proceeding required.

If a person sets up a trust in the will, a *trustee* must be named to administer the trust. A single trustee may be named with alternates as successor trustees. A husband may name his wife as trustee with a son as the alternate trustee upon the wife's death, incapacity, or resignation.

A *guardian* is frequently named if the person has minor children.[34] A guardian of the estate manages any assets the child inherits or acquires. A guardian of the person has physical custody of the child or children. Both require a complicated court proceeding and terminate when the child attains age 18.

Anyone can name a guardian of the estate for a child if the person dies. This is true even if the person is divorced. A guardian of the person usually does not act unless both parents are deceased or cannot act. If a divorced woman has custody of a child and she dies, the child's father has the right to be custodian unless it is determined that he is unfit. If both parents die, a guardian of the child will have to be appointed.

The executor, trustee, and guardian can be different people. Frequently the executor and trustee, who both handle financial tasks, are the same person or persons. The guardian for the child or children may be different depending on which relative or friend will be best for the child or children.

¶513 Signing the Will

A will is signed by the testator before two witnesses. The witnesses should not be people who inherit under the will or who are related to the testator. If an attorney is present, normally the attorney acts as one of the witnesses. The attorney usually asks the person "Now this is your will and you wish us to be witnesses to it?" After the person signs the will, the two witnesses sign.

In California, the statement that the witnesses sign at the end of the will has a standard wording and is signed under a statement that the witnesses declare under "penalty of perjury" that it is correct. If all of the particulars have been done, the will is self-proving and the witnesses do not have to be contacted after the person dies.[35] If no one objects to the will, it is admitted to probate without any later statements from the witnesses.

The attorney may ask that several copies of the will be signed. Possibly only one original will is signed, and then photocopies are made for reference.

¶514 Location of Original Will

What should be done with the original will after it is signed? There are several possibilities. It can be kept at home, left with the attorney, left with a relative such as the person named as executor, or placed in a safe deposit box.

In California, safe deposit boxes are not locked or sealed at death. If there is a cosigner on the box, the cosigner can enter the decedent's box after death and remove the original will. If there is no cosigner on the box and the decedent was

---

[34] California Probate Code section 1501.   [35] California Probate Code section 8220(b).

the only signer, then anyone with a certified copy of the death certificate and a key to the box can enter the box with an officer from the financial institution and remove the original will and burial instructions.[36]

One problem with keeping the original will at home is that it might be difficult to locate the will after death. If it cannot be found and was in the decedent's possession, the presumption is that the decedent voluntarily destroyed the will prior to death. If the will cannot be found, then it cannot be probated or authenticated by the court.

The attorney may hold the will, but that raises a question of ethics since the will is the client's property and he or she should not be required to go back to the attorney to obtain the original will.

Wherever the will is located, it is important that the executor and nearest relatives be aware of the location so that the will can be located quickly after the decedent's death.

¶515 Codicil to a Will

A codicil to a will is a separate legal document executed with the same legal requirements as a will. It may be witnessed by two or more people or handwritten. A person can sign a handwritten or holographic codicil to a witnessed will.

A will should not be changed after it is signed. If the person wishes to change a will, he or she should sign a codicil. The codicil adds to a will, such as a cash bequest; deletes to a will, such as a bequest of a grand piano to a cousin; or changes a provision, such as substituting one child as executor for another child who was named in the will.

Since the will is a separate signed document, the original codicil should be placed with the original will. Any number of codicils can be made to a will. In some cases where the will is short and the codicil or codicils are involved, it may be simpler to draft and sign a new will.

¶516 International Will

The United States, along with most other industrialized countries, has signed a treaty recognizing a will drafted and signed in one country as being valid in all other countries that are parties to this treaty. The requirement for recognition is that a statement be attached to the front of the will and that the will be authenticated by a named official. In California, any attorney licensed to practice law in the State of California may sign this certificate.[37]

Such a certificate is needed when the person who signs the will is moving to another country or owns property in another country.

¶517 Causing Someone's Death

California law, like the laws of most states, prevents anyone who has murdered or caused someone's death from inheriting. Under California law, if someone is convicted of murder or voluntary manslaughter of the decedent, that person cannot inherit. If the person is not criminally tried, it is possible for other

---

[36] California Probate Code section 331.

[37] California Probate Code section 6388.

relatives or beneficiaries under the will, to bring a civil lawsuit and, if successful, prevent the person from inheriting.[38]

The prohibition against inheriting extends not only to a will or intestate succession, but also to other methods of inheritance such as joint tenancy, living trust, or beneficiary designation.

¶518 Summary of Rules of Intestate Succession

MARRIED PERSON

- Community property-all to spouse.

- Quasi-community property-all to spouse.

- Separate property;

— 1/2 to spouse; 1/2 to child.

— 1/3 to spouse; 2/3 to children equally.

— 1/2 to spouse; 1/2 to parents equally or to surviving parent.

— 1/2 to spouse; 1/2 to brothers and sisters.

— All to spouse.

SINGLE PERSON

If a domestic partner survives, the partner receives one-third, one-half, or all of the assets, depending on the relationship of other surviving relatives. The remaining assets, or all of the assets if there is no domestic partner, are distributed as follows:

- Issue, by right of representation.

- Parents equally or to surviving parents.

- Brothers and sisters.

- Grandparents equally or to surviving grandparent or grandparents.

- Issue of grandparents (aunts, uncles and cousins).

- Issue of a predeceased spouse.

- Parents of a predeceased spouse or issue of those parents.

- Next of Kin.

- Next of kin of predeceased spouse.

- State of California.

---

[38] California Probate Code sections 250-258.

Chapter 6

PROBATE

¶600 Introduction

Most people are aware of "probate" but do not know what it means. Especially in view of what is written in the popular media, most people want to avoid the hassle, time, and costs of the probate process.

¶601 Purpose of Probate

Probate is not designed to be an employment bill for attorneys. The probate process can be avoided, but most people do not take the time or effort to understand what the process is and how it can be avoided.

Probate is a legal process whereby a court validates the deceased person's will or determines that he or she died without a will. The court also appoints someone to handle the decedent's assets and pay the bills owed at death. That person is referred to as an executor, administrator, or administrator with the will annexed, depending on the circumstances.

An additional purpose of probate is to see if anyone was owed money at the time of death so that a creditor can come forward and file a claim to receive payment. There is a fixed period of time for creditors to come forward and demand payment.

Along with the payment of debts, the probate process is designed to see that taxes are paid. Income taxes for the personal income tax return up to the date of death must be paid. Income collected during probate requires the filing of a separate estate income tax return and the payment of tax. If the decedent owned over $1,500,000 to $3,500,000 of assets at the date of death, depending on the year of death, a federal estate tax return is required and the tax due must be paid within nine months of the date of death (see Chapter 7 for estate taxes).

Lastly, after all assets of the decedent are collected, assets are sold and taxes and debts are paid, then the executor or administrator must distribute the remaining assets in accordance with the decedent's will or the rules of intestate succession if the decedent died without a will.

¶602 Assets Subject to Probate

While not all assets that the decedent owned are subject to probate, the following assets are subject to the probate process:

1. Assets in the deceased person's name alone.

2. Assets in the decedent's name with his or her spouse, as community property, as to one-half of *each* community property asset (unless the couple has a written agreement to divide assets on a nonprorata basis).

3. The deceased person's portion or share of an asset where the asset is registered as tenants in common with other people.

4. Assets that are owned but are not registered, such as furniture, jewelry, etc.

California law provides that a probate is not necessary if the total value of the assets, at the time of death, which are subject to probate do not exceed the sum of $100,000.[1] There is a simplified procedure for the transfer of these assets.[2] The $100,000 figure does not include vehicles and certain other assets.

¶603 Assets Not Subject to Probate

As mentioned, not everything is subject to probate. Even though there may be a probate for a portion of assets owned, the following assets are not subject to the probate process:

1. Assets held in joint tenancy with another person or persons.

2. Assets held in a living trust.

3. Assets such as life insurance and IRA benefits, where a beneficiary is named.

4. Assets in a bank or savings and loan account in the deceased person's name as "trustee" for someone else.

5. Assets which are registered in a person's name and which are "payable on death" (POD) to someone.

6. Assets which are registered in the person's name and which are "transfer at death" (TAD) to someone.

7. Assets passing to the surviving spouse. If the deceased person owned assets in his or her name alone but these assets are left by will or pass by intestate succession to the surviving spouse.

California has a simplified legal process for assets passing to a surviving spouse, referred to as a "spousal confirmation proceeding." Here, a petition is filed with the court, notice is given to certain parties, and if no one objects, the court approves the assets as going to the spouse. This procedure can only be used for husband and wife.[3]

John Doe has $200,000 of separate property stock in his name alone. He has a will that leaves everything to his wife. His wife can use this spousal confirmation proceeding. The advantage is no fixed fee like there is for probate, and the process takes approximately 60 days instead of 9-12 months.

¶604 Steps Involved in the Probate Process

When someone dies, the first question is whether there will be a probate proceeding. If all of the assets are in a living trust or joint tenancy, there will not be a probate proceeding. If the deceased person has more than $100,000 of assets

[1] California Probate Code section 13100.
[2] California Probate Code section 13101.
[3] California Probate Code sections 13650-13660.

in his or her name alone and there is no surviving spouse or the assets were not left to the spouse, then there will be a probate proceeding.

If it is necessary to have probate, the second question is who will act? If the decedent left a will, he or she named someone in the will as executor. That person or persons does not have to be a California or United States citizen or resident. A friend may serve, his or her three children may jointly serve, or a California bank or trust company may serve. No one who is named as executor has to serve. The person or bank can decline to act.

If there is no will, the nearest relative or relatives have the first right to serve as administrator or to nominate someone to act if they do not wish to serve.[4] If there is no will, the person appointed by the court is called an administrator.

Occasionally, someone will die with a will, but the will does not name an executor or the person named is deceased or will not serve. Or possibly a bank is named and the bank declines because the estate is not large enough. The court then appoints the nearest relative who inherits under the will.[5] That person is referred to as an administrator with the will annexed.

All of the above persons do the same duty once they get appointed even though their title varies depending upon the circumstances.

.01 Appointment by Court

To start the probate process it is necessary to file a petition with the superior court in the county where the deceased person lived at the time of death. This petition is set for hearing approximately 30-60 days after it is filed with the court.[6] A filing fee is paid, which can range from approximately $250 to $4,000 or more, depending upon the value of the assets probated.

If there is an emergency and it is necessary for someone to act prior to the court hearing, it is possible to get someone appointed within 24 hours as a "special administrator."[7] This person handles estate assets until the executor or administrator is appointed. If the decedent was the only signer on a business bank account and salary and other bills have to be paid immediately, a special administrator can be appointed.

After the petition is filed, a notice of the court hearing must be published three times in a local newspaper.[8] In addition, a notice of the court hearing must be mailed at least 15 days prior to the hearing to everyone named in the will, all of the deceased person's heirs at law (those people who would inherit if he or she died without a will), and any alternate executors named in the will.[9]

If the will had special wording at the end, where the witnesses sign, then it may be "self-proving" and no additional statements are necessary. If the will is not self-proving then a statement must be obtained from one of the witnesses of the will.[10] If a witness cannot be located, then there are several alternative ways

---

[4] California Probate Code section 8465.

[5] California Probate Code section 8441.

[6] California Probate Code section 8003.

[7] California Probate Code sections 8540-8547.

[8] California Probate Code sections 8120-8125.

[9] California Probate Code section 8110.

[10] California Probate Code sections 8220-8221.

of proving the will. If the will is handwritten, anyone who is familiar with the decedent's handwriting can sign a statement proving the will.[11]

If the will does not waive a surety bond, then the executor or administrator must post a surety bond.[12] The surety bond is nothing more than an insurance policy which insures the estate if the executor or administrator does something improper or steals from the estate. Unfortunately, a premium can be $200-5,000 depending upon the value of the assets in the estate.

At the court hearing if everything has been done and there are no objections, the court will admit the will to probate and appoint the executor or administrator.

After the appointment, the executor or administrator must file a special form with the court titled "letters testamentary" or "letters of administration." The person then signs this form, and he or she agrees to act as executor or administrator. Later, when taking legal action or transferring assets, other parties will want a certified copy of these "letters" showing that the person has the legal authority to act.

.02 Collecting Assets

After the appointment, the executor or administrator must take possession of all of the decedent's assets subject to the probate process. Assets in joint tenancy, assets in a living trust, or assets subject to a beneficiary designation are not part of the probate and are not collected.

The executor or administrator needs to change title to the assets and to put these assets in his or her name as executor or administrator. Mutual funds, stocks and bonds, brokerage accounts, bank accounts, real property, vehicles, and other assets should be changed over.

After collecting all of the assets, it is necessary to prepare an inventory listing these assets.[13] At the time that the executor or administrator is appointed, the court also appoints a "California Probate Referee." This individual has the responsibility of valuing all of the non-cash items with the fair market value as of the date of death. The referee receives a fee of $1 per $1000 for the value of the assets appraised. The value is the gross value excluding any loans or liens on the assets. If the home is valued at $300,000, even though there is an $180,000 mortgage on this home, the referee values it at $300,000 and receives a $300 fee for the appraisal.

There are legal procedures for contesting the referee's value if someone does not believe it to be accurate.

The appraisal of all of the assets is supposed to be filed with the court within four months of the executor's or administrator's appointment.

---

[11] California Probate Code section 8222.
[12] California Probate Code sections 8480-8482.

[13] California Probate Code sections 8800-8804.

.03 Payment of Bills and Debts

As soon as the executor or administrator is appointed by the court and obtains funds, bills can be paid. Funeral, utility, credit card, and other bills can be paid without any special legal formality.

Anyone can be required to submit a creditor's claim in the estate. This is a special court form which must be completed by the creditor and approved by the executor or administrator. If the executor or administrator wants this form submitted by a creditor, then a notice must be sent to the creditor.

Claims normally must be submitted within four months of the executor or administrator's appointment.[14] There is an exception if the creditor was not aware of the death. If that occurs, the creditor can petition the court after the four month period for submitting a claim. The petition cannot be filed later than one year after the executor or administrator's appointment.[15]

If the executor or administrator rejects a creditor's claim, the creditor must file a lawsuit within three months of the rejection or lose all right to later sue.[16] Before a lawsuit can be filed, the creditor must file a claim.[17]

If John Doe is in an automobile accident and dies, and other parties wish to sue his estate, they must file a creditor's claim within the required period before they can file a lawsuit.

Most estates do not involve any creditor's claims. The executor or administrator frequently pays the outstanding bills and no one objects.

.04 Sale of Estate Assets

It may be necessary or practical to sell some or all of the estate assets. Assets may have to be sold to pay taxes, fees, and debts. Or the home may be vacant and the children do not wish to inherit it, so it is sold during probate.

There are two methods of selling assets in a probate proceeding the executor or administrator may chose.

First, court approval may be obtained before any asset is sold.[18] If stocks or bonds are sold, a court order is necessary before selling them. If real estate is sold, a court hearing must be held and anyone may offer a higher price for the property in court and take it away from the original buyer.

Second, the executor or administrator may sell assets under a provision of California law referred to as the "Independent Administration of Estates Act."[19] Under this act the executor or administrator may sell any asset. The only requirement is to give written notice to any beneficiary who is affected by the sale at least 15 days before the proposed date of sale. If no one objects, then the sale may proceed. If someone objects, then the court must be petitioned for approval the same as alternative number one.

---

[14] California Probate Code section 9100.
[15] California Probate Code section 9103.
[16] California Probate Code section 9353.
[17] California Probate Code section 9370.
[18] California Probate Code section 10006.
[19] California Probate Code sections 10500-10592.

After appointment, the executor or administrator usually prepares a budget with an estimate of the federal estate tax, fees for the executor and attorney, administrative costs, cash bequests under the will, and debts or claims. If there is insufficient cash available, then a decision must be made as to what assets to sell. If there is sufficient cash available, then a decision must be made as to whether any assets such as the home should be sold.

Once the decision is made to sell assets, the executor or administrator should proceed with the sale. It makes little sense to allow the home to remain vacant for nine months and then put it on the market for sale. If the home is going to be sold, there seems little reason why it should not be marketed within approximately 30 days of appointment.

.05 Payment of Taxes

The executor or administrator is liable to make sure that all of the taxes due the federal government and the State of California are paid. While he is not normally personally liable, his liability does extend to the assets that are in probate. If the executor or administrator distributes assets and the Internal Revenue Service or California Franchise Tax Board assesses a deficiency, he is liable to the value of the assets distributed.

One immediate concern is who will handle all of the tax work involved? It can be the executor or administrator if the person is skilled enough to do so. Or, it may be the attorney. More likely it will be the tax preparer, enrolled agent, or certified public accountant that handled the decedent's tax matters prior to death. Whoever is chosen to do this must be skilled enough to prepare and file all of the required tax returns.

Federal Estate Tax. The federal estate tax or "death" tax is discussed in detail in chapter 7. If a person dies with over $1,500,000 to $3,500,000 in assets, depending on the year of death, an estate tax return must be filed within nine months of the decedent's death.[20] An extension to file this return may be obtained for up to an additional six months.[21]

Any amounts left to qualified charities and any amounts left to the decedent's spouse (if a United States citizen) are exempt. All debts that the decedent owed at the time of death such as funeral costs, legal fees, debts, etc. are also deducted. If the net estate is over this exemption after deducting the debts a tax of 45-49% of the amount over the exemption is payable.[22] If the return is not filed within the required time limit or if the tax due is not paid there may be substantial penalties and interest. Because the value of the assets is the value as of the date of death, the person who is preparing the tax needs to immediately start gathering information after the decedent's death.

Prior to Death Income Tax Returns. Even when someone dies, an income tax return has to be filed for the year of death. Mary Doe dies on July 21st. An income tax return will be required from the first of the year until the date of death-January 1st-July 21st.[23] The return is due by April 15th of the following

---

[20] Internal Revenue Code section 6075(a).
[21] Internal Revenue Code section 6081(a).
[22] Internal Revenue Code section 2010(c).
[23] Internal Revenue Code section 6101.

year. Only the income received and any deductions paid through the date of death will be reported on the return. Income, such as dividends and interest, received after the date of death will not be reported on the return but will be picked up on the estate income tax return or by the surviving joint tenant, if the asset was in joint tenancy.

Any medical deductions on the decedent's part paid within one year of the date of death may be deducted on the final return.[24] All other deductions must have been paid before death to be allowable.

Estimated income taxes paid for the year of death should be reviewed. Depending upon the date of death, it may not be necessary to continue to make estimated payments after death.

The decedent's income tax returns for the four years prior to death should be retained and the return for the year prior to death should be carefully reviewed to be sure all items of income and deductions are picked up.

If the decedent died after January 1st but before April 15th or even later, a return may still be due for the prior year. With extensions, it is possible to file the income tax return as late as October 15th for the prior year. If the return has not yet been filed, an extension can be requested and will usually be granted.

Fiduciary Income Tax Returns. Income that comes in after the date of death is not reported on the decedent's personal income tax return. If the interest, dividends, or other income are paid to the estate, they must be reported on the fiduciary or estate income tax return. A separate tax identification number is obtained for the estate and used in lieu of the decedent's social security number.

A separate income tax return, called a fiduciary tax return, is filed annually for the estate.[25] This form lists the taxable income such as dividends, interest, capital gains, and net rents. The fiduciary return also takes off the allowable deductions such as mortgage interest, legal and executor's fees, taxes, and a few other deductions.

The tax return does not have to be filed on a calendar year basis, as of December 31st. It can be filed on a fiscal year basis at the end of any calendar month.[26] Once a fiscal year is picked, the return must be filed within 3-1/2 months of the end of the tax year.[27]

At the end of the tax year, if the estate has not been closed and distributed, the tax is then paid on the net income. That income is later distributed to the beneficiaries of the estate without additional tax. If the estate has been distributed during the tax year, the tax is not paid on the net income, but instead each beneficiary must list his or her proportionate share of the taxable income on his or her personal tax return.

Fiduciary tax returns are required until the estate is closed and distributed. If the estate is open for more than two tax years, estimated fiduciary taxes must be paid each year.

---

[24] Internal Revenue Code section 213(c).
[25] Internal Revenue Code section 6012(a)(3).
[26] Internal Revenue Code section 7701(a)(24).
[27] Internal Revenue Code section 6072(a).

Other Taxes. Other taxes may also be due. Real estate taxes are due in California by December 10th and April 10th.[28] Sales tax may be due if there is a business selling some product.

If the decedent made a gift of over $11,000 to someone during the year of death, a gift tax return may be due.[29] If there is real property in another state or country, it may be necessary to file a separate income tax return for the income in that state or country.

Liability for Taxes. As previously mentioned, the executor is liable for taxes if assets are distributed and additional taxes are later discovered to be due.[30] Because of this, the executor or administrator will frequently request to hold back some estate funds for a period of time as a reserve in case additional taxes are due. This reserve may be kept for two to three years and then distributed without an additional court order.

The period of liability for taxes is normally three years for the federal government.[31] This period is from the due date of the return or the filing date if it is later. The period of liability for the State of California for income tax returns is four years.[32] The liability for a 2003 return filed on or before April 15, 2004, will expire on April 15, 2007 for the Internal Revenue Service, and on April 15, 2008 for the California Franchise Tax Board. There are longer periods of liability if the taxes are underpaid by 25% or more. The period of liability never runs out if a tax return is not filed or if there is fraud involved.

.06 Concluding the Estate

The estate can be distributed after the estate assets have been inventoried, the period for filing creditor's claims has expired and all claims paid or resolved, the necessary assets sold, and all required tax returns filed and taxes due paid.

To conclude the estate, it is necessary to petition the court and obtain a court order to make the distribution. The executor must either file an elaborate accounting listing all receipts and disbursements or obtain a waiver of the accounting from all of the estate beneficiaries.

After the accounting is prepared or waived, a petition is drafted to summarize what has happened in the estate and the actions taken. This petition lists the assets currently on hand and the proposed distribution of these assets. The statutory fees that the executor or administrator and the attorney receive is computed and shown.

If everything is in order and there are no objections, the court will issue an order concluding the estate, ordering the fees paid, and the assets distributed.

Once the court order is obtained, checks may be written and assets reregistered in the names of the estate beneficiaries. After the assets are distributed, a receipt for these assets is obtained from each estate beneficiary and filed with the court.

---

[28] California Revenue & Taxation Code sections 2617-2618.

[29] Internal Revenue Code section 2503(b).

[30] Internal Revenue Code section 6901(a)(1)(B).

[31] Internal Revenue Code section 6501(a).

[32] California Revenue & Taxation Code section 19057(a).

As previously stated, if the estate is relatively simple and no federal estate tax is due, it can be concluded in six to nine months. If there is an estate tax due, the period will likely increase to 12-15 months. The estate should not be in probate for more than 18 months unless there is litigation or significant problems that prevent distribution.

.07 Executor's and Attorney's Fees

The fee paid an executor or administrator and an attorney for probate in California is set by law and is a percentage of the estate. Either party can waive all or a portion of the fixed or statutory fee and take a smaller amount.

The fee is computed on a fee base. This fee base is the value of the inventory filed for the estate assets, income that has come in during the period of probate, and any capital gains on the sale of estate assets less any capital losses on the sale of any estate assets. If an accounting is waived, the fee base is only the inventory value.

The fee base is then applied to a percentage fee structure.[33]

	ESTATE VALUE	FEE	CUMULATIVE FEE
4% of the first	$ 100,000	$ 4,000	$ 4,000
3% of the next	$ 100,000	$ 3,000	$ 7,000
2% of the next	$ 800,000	$ 16,000	$ 23,000
1% of the next	$ 9,000,000	$ 90,000	$ 113,000
1/2 of 1% of the next	$ 15,000,000	$ 75,000	$ 188,000

The court determines the amount of the fee for the excess over $25,000,000 of value.

The fee paid *each* to the executor or administrator and to the attorney for various size estates are as follows:

ESTATE VALUE	FEE
$ 100,000	$ 4,000
$ 200,000	$ 7,000
$ 300,000	$ 9,000
$ 400,000	$ 11,000
$ 500,000	$ 13,000
$ 600,000	$ 15,000
$ 700,000	$ 17,000
$ 800,000	$ 19,000
$ 900,000	$ 21,000
$ 1,000,000	$ 23,000

In addition, either the executor, administrator, the attorney, or both, may request extraordinary fees for services above these amounts.[34] Additional compensation will generally be awarded by the court for preparing and filing any tax returns, selling the decedent's assets (including real property), litigation, continuing the decedent's business, and various other matters. The amount requested varies depending upon the amount of time involved and is subject to the court's discretion.

[33] California Probate Code sections 10800 and 10810.

[34] California Probate Code sections 10801 and 10811.

Chapter 7

FEDERAL ESTATE AND GENERATION- SKIPPING TRANSFER TAXES

¶700 Introduction

One of the most important considerations in estate planning is the potential "death taxes" that will be imposed on the decedent's assets at death. Because of the high tax rates, it is necessary to see if any planning can be done to reduce or eliminate these taxes.

¶701 Nature of Estate Tax

The federal estate tax is a death tax that was originally imposed in 1916 to raise additional revenue in connection with Word War I. Over the years it has been changed significantly. Between the World Wars, the rates increased from 25% to a maximum of 60%. Prior to 1981, spouses were not exempt, so that if either husband or wife died there frequently was a tax. This was eliminated in 1982, and modified in 1988 so that if the surviving spouse is not a United States citizen the exemption from tax is no longer available.

The estate tax exemption has increased over the years. Originally it was $60,000 in the early 70s, increased to $175,000 in the late 70s and, under President Ronald Reagan, was raised in steps to $600,000. In the late 1990s the exemption was increased over a number of years, designed to rise from $600,000 to $1,000,000. In 2001, the latest set of changes passed, increasing the exemption in steps to $3,500,000 in 2009, abolishing the estate tax in 2010, and then having it possibly reappear with a $1,000,000 exemption in 2011.

The tax is imposed on the assets of the decedent. Any assets that the decedent owned are subject to this estate tax based on the fair market value of the assets at the date of death.[1]

If the decedent is a United States citizen or a permanent resident, the tax is imposed on all assets owned anywhere in the world.[2] Even if another country should impose a tax on the same assets, they are taxed by the United States.

Currently, the first $1,500,000 of assets is exempt from tax, with this exemption rising in future years to $3,500,000. The excess is taxed at a starting rate of 45%. The maximum estate tax rate, which previously was at 55% with a 5% surcharge in some cases, has declined to 48%, and will decline lower in future

[1] Internal Revenue Code section 2031(a).   [2] Internal Revenue Code section 2001(a).

years to a maximum of 45%. By 2007 we will have a flat tax of 45% on all assets over the exemption amount

¶702 Requirements for Filing a Return

A return is required in many cases even though no tax is due. If the total value of all of the decedent's assets exceeds $1,500,000 to $3,500,000, depending upon the year of death and based on the value of all assets as of the date of death, a return must be filed within nine months of the date of death.[3] This value does not take into account any deductions or any amounts left the surviving spouse or a charity. All of the decedent's assets including pension plans, life insurance, and IRA account are subject to tax.

If the return cannot be filed within the nine month period, an extension can be requested for an additional six months, allowing a maximum of 15 months to file the return.[4]

If the return is filed late without an extension, there is a penalty of 5% per month or any fraction of a month that the return is late, up to a maximum of 25%.[5] Filing a return even one day late will incur a penalty of 5%. There is also a penalty of 1/2 of 1% per month for filing a return but not paying the tax due with the return. Again the maximum penalty for late payment is 25%.[6] The Internal Revenue Service also charges interest on all late tax payments.[7] The interest is adjusted periodically by the service and is currently approximately 7% per year.

The federal tax form is Form 706, with the instructions to the return published separately. This form is currently reprinted annually and if a return is being prepared, the current version must be used.

The filing requirements depending upon the year of death are:

- 2004—$1,500,000
- 2005—$1,500,000
- 2006—$2,000,000
- 2007—$2,000,000
- 2008—$2,000,000
- 2009—$3,500,000
- 2010—Exempt-no estate tax
- 2011—$1,000,000

¶703 Valuation of Assets

All assets which the deceased person owned are valued at their fair market value as of the date of death.[8] Fair market value is the price for which you could sell the asset. For example, furniture is valued at its sale value, not its replacement value.

---

[3] Internal Revenue Code section 6075(a).
[4] Internal Revenue Code section 6081(a).
[5] Internal Revenue Code section 6651(a)(1).

[6] Internal Revenue Code section 6651(a)(2).
[7] Internal Revenue Code section 6601.
[8] Internal Revenue Service regulation 20.2031-1(b).

Traded securities such as stocks and bonds are valued at the average between the high and the low price as of the date of death. If the person died on a weekend when the market is closed, the securities must be valued at the average between the high and low for both Friday and Monday, and these two figures averaged.

Real estate is valued at its sale price. If the property is sold within a year of the date of death, the gross sales price is normally accepted as the value at date of death. The government will not allow the estate to deduct selling costs of real property such as real estate commission and closing costs unless the property must be sold to raise funds to pay the estate tax, cash bequests, debts, and expenses.

The value of furniture, furnishings, and jewelry is generally low, such as $5,000-10,000 for all of the items.

Bank accounts are valued at the current balance. Notes owed the decedent are also valued at the principal balance due at date of death.

Assets can be valued at one of two dates. They can all be valued at the date of death or all at an "alternate valuation date."[9] The alternate valuation date is six months from the date of death. If the assets have a lower value six months later, then the lower value can be used. The alternate valuation date value can only be used if it lessens the value of the estate and decreases the amount of tax due.

If any assets are sold or transferred within the six month period and do not exist six months after death, then for alternate valuation purposes, these assets are valued at the sales price or value on the date of transfer.

Any assets that do not change in terms of market value have the same value on the alternate date as on the date of death. A bank account will have the same value for both dates since there is no change other than interest after death. U. S. Savings Bonds, notes due the decedent, and a few other assets do not change in value.

All assets have to be valued on the date of death or six months later. A value cannot be picked on one date for some assets and another date for others.

¶704 Deductions

Deductions are allowed for all debts of the decedent and for all expenses at death.[10] This would include funeral and burial costs, all legal, accounting and probate costs, debts of the decedent for anything owed at the time of death, unpaid medical expenses owed at death, costs of maintaining assets such as utilities and a gardener for the home, and any losses if an asset is destroyed after death without adequate insurance.

Anything left to a qualified charity is also deductible.[11] To qualify, the charity must be located in the United States and cash or assets must pass to the charity at the decedent's direction at death. If John Doe left $10,000 to his local

---

[9] Internal Revenue Code section 2032.
[10] Internal Revenue Code section 2053.

[11] Internal Revenue Code section 2055.

college at death, this would be deductible. If the relatives voluntarily give $10,000 to the charity after his death, this would not be deductible.

Any amounts left voluntarily to the federal government, a political subdivision of the federal government, any state, or subdivision of a state, are also deductible.[12]

¶705 Marital Deduction

Since 1982, any amount left to a person's spouse is exempt from taxation.[13] A 1988 change required that the surviving spouse be a United states citizen (residency is not sufficient) for this exemption to apply.[14] Provided the spouse is a United states citizen, then any amount may be left estate tax free to the spouse. Generally, there is no estate tax on the death of the first spouse. There is no limit on the amount that may be left to the spouse. Husband and wife may have a $20,000,000 estate and on the first death, if everything is left to the surviving spouse and the spouse is a United States citizen, it all is exempt from estate taxation.

This marital deduction may be obtained in a number of ways.

Assets may be left outright to the spouse. This means that the assets pass without restrictions. It may be by joint tenancy, beneficiary designation, living trust and will, or intestate succession.

The second method is to use one of several types of trusts. A *marital deduction trust*[15] is an irrevocable trust where the surviving spouse receives all of the income from the trust and at the surviving spouse's death, he or she has the right to leave the trust assets to anyone the surviving spouse wishes.

A *qualified terminable interest trust*[16] sometimes referred to as a "Q-Tip" trust, is also an irrevocable trust. The surviving spouse receives all of the income for life but when the surviving spouse dies the assets are not controlled by the surviving spouse but by the first spouse's designation regarding who receives these assets.

A *qualified domestic trust*[17] is used where the surviving spouse is not a United States citizen. Here, an irrevocable trust is set up for the surviving spouse and he or she receives all of the income for life. One of the trustees must be a United States citizen and the trust must stay in the United States. Other specific rules apply.

John and Mary Doe have $4,000,000 of community property assets. John Doe dies in 2004 and his one-half of the community property is $2,000,000. He can do anything he wishes with $1,500,000, but to avoid tax on the additional $500,000 he must take advantage of the marital deduction. Provided his wife is a United States citizen he can leave $500,000 to her outright, put it in a marital deduction trust which she can control in terms of who inherits it when she dies, or put it in an qualified terminable interest trust which she cannot control at death.

---

[12] Internal Revenue Code section 2055.

[13] Internal Revenue Code section 2056.

[14] Internal Revenue Code section 2056(d).

[15] Internal Revenue Code section 2056(b)(5).

[16] Internal Revenue Code section 2056(b)(7)(B).

[17] Internal Revenue Code section 2056A.

If he leaves this excess to other people or leaves it in another irrevocable trust, it will be taxed when he dies. In all other cases where he utilizes the marital deduction, the assets are not taxed on the husband's death but are taxed when the wife later dies.

¶706 Tax Rates

The tax rates are based on the decedent's "taxable estate." This is the total value of all the assets minus all deductions, including amounts left to charities and the marital deduction for assets left to the spouse. This net figure is referred to as the taxable estate and the gross estate tax is computed on this amount. The tax rate is based on the following schedule.[18]

$1,500,000-$2,000,000	45% tax rate
Over $2,000,000	Flat rate on excess of 48% (for 2004)

This maximum rate decreases 1% per year as follows:
- 2005—47%
- 2006—46%
- 2007 and subsequent years—45%[19]

¶707 Unified Tax Credit

To make life more confusing, the federal estate tax is not simple in its calculation. It is computed by taking the taxable estate (assets less deductions) and computing a tax on this net amount without an exemption.[20] The federal government then gives the estate an estate tax credit for the equivalent of the exemption.[21]

John Doe dies in 2004 with assets of $2,200,000 and deductions of $200,000. His taxable estate is $2,000,000. Instead of applying the exemption, the tax is determined on the full $2,000,000. This gross estate tax is $780,800. However, a tax credit is allowed for the estate tax on $1,500,000 ($555,800), which is the exemption for 2004. The estate tax payable is the difference of $225,000. This works out the same as applying the tax rate of 45% to the $500,000 difference ($2,000,000-$1,500,000).

¶708 Federal Estate Taxes Due

To simplify matters, the "net" amount of federal estate tax due for various size estates is as follows, depending upon the year of death:

[18] Internal Revenue Code section 2001(c).
[19] Internal Revenue Code section 2001(c)(2).
[20] Internal Revenue Code section 2001(c).
[21] Internal Revenue Code section 2010.

Year of Death	2004	2005	2006	2007	2008	2009
Exemption	1,500,000	1,500,000	2,000,000	2,000,000	2,000,000	3,500,000
Taxable Estate			Amount of Tax Payable			
1,500,000	0	0	0	0	0	0
1,600,000	45,000	45,000	0	0	0	0
1,700,000	90,000	90,000	0	0	0	0
1,800,000	135,000	135,000	0	0	0	0
1,900,000	180,000	180,000	0	0	0	0
2,000,000	225,000	225,000	0	0	0	0
2,100,000	273,000	272,000	46,000	45,000	45,000	0
2,200,000	321,000	319,000	92,000	90,000	90,000	0
2,300,000	369,000	366,000	138,000	135,000	135,000	0
2,400,000	417,000	413,000	184,000	180,000	180,000	0
2,500,000	465,000	460,000	230,000	225,000	225,000	0
2,600,000	513,000	507,000	276,000	270,000	270,000	0
2,700,000	561,000	554,000	322,000	315,000	315,000	0
2,800,000	609,000	601,000	368,000	360,000	360,000	0
2,900,000	657,000	648,000	414,000	405,000	405,000	0
3,000,000	705,000	695,000	460,000	450,000	450,000	0

On estates of over $3,000,000, the excess over $3,000,000 ($3,500,000 in 2009) is taxed at the following percentage rate:

| 48% | 47% | 46% | 45% | 45% | 45% |

¶709 Special Valuation of Assets

There are special provisions for a lower than normal valuation for certain assets. Assets consisting of a ranch, farm, or closely held business real estate, may be valued at a lower valuation if it has been used in a family business and continues to be held and used by family members for up to 15 years after death. If sold or disposed of during the 15-year period, then all or a portion of the reduced taxes must be repaid.[22]

There are a number of technical provisions with regard to this lower valuation.

¶710 Deferral of Payment of Tax

If the estate lacks liquidity to pay the estate tax due, it may defer payment of the tax for up to 10 years.[23] This tax must be paid in installments and interest is charged at the prevailing IRS interest rate.

If the estate consisted of $3,000,000 of real estate and no other assets, the tax of $705,000 may be deferred. The IRS will place a lien on the properties and if the real property is sold, the tax must be paid from the proceeds of any sale.

---

[22] Internal Revenue Code section 2032A.   [23] Internal Revenue Code section 6161(a).

¶711 Audit of Estate Tax Return

After the return is filed, the Internal Revenue Service has three years from the due date, or from the filing date, whichever is later, to audit the estate.[24] Every estate tax return is reviewed and a decision is made to audit or not audit the estate.

Usually a decision to audit or accept the return is made within 8-12 months after the return is filed.

If the estate tax return is not audited, an "estate tax closing letter" is sent to the taxpayer accepting the return as filed. If the return is audited, the IRS sends a personal letter to the taxpayer asking for a meeting and requesting additional information. Audits are generally made where there are questions as to the valuation of assets, particularly real property and business interests. Other considerations would include transfers of assets before death such as life insurance or other high value items, or questions regarding deductions taken on the return.

If there is an audit and an agreement, the taxpayer will be asked to sign an agreement increasing the tax. If there is no agreement, the Internal Revenue Service may assess a deficiency and the taxpayer has the right to appeal this notice and to take the matter to tax court. If there is a tax deficiency, the government will bill the taxpayer for the balance of the tax due plus interest and penalties.

¶712 State Death Tax Credit

The federal government gives the state in which the taxpayer lived a portion of the estate tax. The Internal Revenue Service does not send this but the taxpayer must complete a state form, mail a check to the state in which the decedent resided at the time of death, and deduct this amount from the estate tax payable to the federal government.

This tax credit runs from 4.8% of the taxable estate to 16% for estates over $9,980,000.

California has a one-page estate tax form, Form ET-1, which is completed and mailed to the California Controller in Sacramento along with a copy of the estate tax return. The tax is deducted from the IRS portion so that it does not increase the total that the taxpayer pays.[25]

As a result of the federal estate tax changes in 2001, this tax is being phased out. The states will receive 25% of the above for 2004, but starting in 2005 and for future years this tax credit will disappear.[26] The states will lose about three billion dollars of revenue from this source and the IRS will take an increased amount of this estate tax representing this credit.

---

[24] Internal Revenue Code section 6501(a).
[25] Internal Revenue Code section 2011.

[26] Internal Revenue Code section 2011(b)(2)(B).

¶713 Foreign Death Taxes

If the decedent owned foreign assets consisting of real estate in another country or stock of a corporation organized in another country, those assets may be taxed by the other country and also by the United States. The United States has estate tax treaties with many countries as to which country gets to tax assets and the credit given by the other country for taxes paid in both countries.[27] If there is no treaty, then there are provisions under the Internal Revenue Code for a partial or full credit for taxes paid.[28]

John Doe is a United States citizen but owns property in France. France imposes a death tax on this property. The United States taxes the same real estate in France since John Doe is a United States citizen. A credit will be allowed on the United States estate tax return. The credit may not be for the full amount paid the foreign government but is based on a formula and can be less than that paid France.

¶714 Cost Basis of Assets at Death

If assets are subject to the federal estate tax at death, these assets get a new value for income tax purposes.[29] John Doe dies and owns 100 shares of XYZ stock. The stock originally cost him $3,000 but is worth $10,000 at the date of death. For income tax purposes the stock gets a new value. If the stock is sold, then the basis for determining capital gains or loss is not the original cost but the value at the date of death-$10,000.

This new valuation is generally beneficial since it eliminates all capital gains on the assets at death. Many people have stocks and real estate that have increased in value since purchase. If they were sold prior to death, a large capital gains tax would be due. If they are kept until death all capital gains would be eliminated and the assets would be revalued for income tax purposes.

If a federal estate tax return is filed, the new value is the value listed on the federal estate tax return. This would either be the value on the date of death or the alternate value if that value were used.

If no federal estate tax return is required because the estate is below the current estate tax exemption, the assets still get a new value based on the fair market value as of the date of death.

If the assets are not subject to federal estate tax, such as in an irrevocable trust, then they do not get a new value for income tax purposes.

For California income tax purposes, if the assets get a new value for federal income tax purposes, the State also allows a new value.[30]

¶715 Generation-Skipping Transfer Tax

The Tax Reform Act of 1986 added another tax structure with regard to "generation-skipping" transfers.[31] These provisions were added to correct the situation where a person died and established a trust. The assets were taxed at

---

[27] Internal Revenue Code section 2014.
[28] Internal Revenue Code section 2014(b).
[29] Internal Revenue Code section 1014.

[30] California Revenue & Taxation Code section 18151.
[31] Internal Revenue Code section 2601.

the person's death but the trust could run for the lifetime of the children and, in some cases, for the lifetime of the grandchildren, and not be taxed again. Since the child did not own the trust assets, there was no estate tax on these assets when the child died. To avoid estate taxes, wealthy people were setting up these generation-skipping trusts.

These provisions apply to an irrevocable transfer of assets or a trust that becomes irrevocable on or after October 22, 1986. Trusts that were irrevocable or where the trust creator died before that date are exempt.

A generation-skipping transfer occurs when assets are transferred to a second generation such as grandchildren. This can be a direct skip, where assets are left directly to a grandchild, or an indirect skip, where a trust is established for a child and upon the child's death the assets pass to the grandchildren.

The exemption from this generation-skipping transfer tax is computed after the federal estate tax is paid. Depending upon the year of death, the generation-skipping transfer tax exemption per decedent is now identical to the estate tax exemption. The tax rate is the maximum federal estate tax rate in effect for the year of death.

Year	Exemption	Tax rate
2004	$1,500,000	48%
2005	$1,500,000	47%
2006	$2,000,000	46%
2007	$2,000,000	45%
2008	$2,000,000	45%
2009	$3,500,000	45%

The above exemption is per decedent,[32] so that husband and wife can pass twice the above exemptions, if correctly structured, to grandchildren without tax.

If a child dies before the parent, there is an exemption since the grandchildren (children of that child) move up and become the next generation.

It is extremely important to structure estate plans which are involved in generation-skipping planning to fully utilize the $1,500,000 to $3,500,000 exemption for each party. It is also a requirement to identify the exempt assets so that the future growth on these assets will also be exempt. Careful planning is very important in view of the 45% future top tax rate.

---

[32] Internal Revenue Code sections 2631(c) and 2643(d).

Chapter 8

GIFTS

¶800 Introduction

The federal government has a gift tax structure, since without a gift tax people would be able to give away most or all of their assets before death and avoid the federal estate tax.

Prior to 1982, there was a separate gift tax structure. People making gifts frequently paid a gift tax but they removed assets from the top estate tax bracket (which went up to 70%) and paid tax at a starting rate of approximately 10-15%. This was abolished in 1982, and the two structures were put together in a "unified tax system." Under this system the taxable gifts are taken into account when a person dies and the federal estate tax is imposed.

There are a number of exceptions to the gift tax, and in doing any planning, people should understand the gift tax system and be aware of the advantages and disadvantages of making gifts.

¶801 Valuation of Assets

The value of assets, for gift tax purposes, is the fair market value as of the date of gift.[1] This is what an asset may be sold for on that date. If a person gives 100 shares of stock to his son and the stock is selling for $15 per share on the date of gift, the value of the gift is $1,500. The income tax basis for the stock is separate.

¶802 Annual Exemption

Every person may give up to $11,000 of cash and assets based on fair market value at the date of gift to each recipient or donee each calendar year.[2] The annual gift tax exemption prior to 2003 was $10,000 a year per donee. Mary Doe, a widow, has three children. She may give $11,000 to each child each year. Collectively she may give $33,000 per year to the three children, and over a five-year period this would amount to $165,000. These gifts are exempt from gift tax and no gift tax return is required if the amount does not exceed $11,000 a year per donee or recipient.

The gifts do not have to be made to family members but can be made to anyone. Gifts, like an inheritance, are not subject to income tax.[3] There is no income tax deduction for the donor and no income tax to report by the recipient.

---

[1] Internal Revenue Code section 2512(a).
[2] Internal Revenue Code section 2503(b)(2).
[3] Internal Revenue Code section 102(a).

The only exception for income taxation is installment obligations (where the capital gain was deferred), United States savings bonds, and single premium deferred annuities. The gift of these items will give rise to an income tax liability for the *donor* but not for the donee. A person should not make a gift of these items without discussing the tax implications with an accountant or attorney.

The $11,000 per year gift tax exemption is only allowed for gifts that meet the requirement of being a gift by what the Internal Revenue Code refers to as a "present interest."[4] This means that the recipient receives the gift immediately without restriction, or it is restricted until the donee attains age 21. If a couple wishes to set up a trust for their children with each child receiving assets at age 30, the gifts will not be "present interest" gifts and will not qualify for the $11,000 exemption.

¶803 Educational and Medical Payments

In addition to the $11,000 per year exemption, an individual can also pay certain bills. These amounts are unlimited and do not impact or reduce the ability to give someone $11,000 per year.

First, education costs in terms of tuition can be paid in any amount, provided that the payments are made directly to the educational institution.[5] This does not include books, room and board, travel, or any payments other than tuition.

Mary Doe discovers that her granddaughter has been accepted to Stanford University. Rather than give her son and daughter-in-law $22,000 per year to pay the girl's costs, Mary may pay the University directly for the tuition. She can also give her granddaughter up to $11,000 per year in gifts, and make gifts of $22,000 per year to her son and daughter-in-law.

Second, medical costs of virtually any type can be paid provided that payment is made directly to the provider of the medical service.[6] Mary Doe pays her son and daughter-in-law's medical insurance of $1,000 per quarter by sending a check directly to the medical insurance company.

Medical costs are defined as anything that would be deductible if the person had paid it as an itemized deduction on his or her income tax return. This includes doctor, hospital, medical insurance, prescription drugs, ambulance, and numerous other services. Again, this does not reduce the ability to give the person $11,000 per year.

¶804 Marital Deduction

A person may give any amount, tax free, to a spouse provided the spouse is a United States citizen. John Doe has $1,000,000 of separate property. He decides to make this $1,000,000 community property, which means that he is giving one-half or $500,000 to his wife, who is a U.S. citizen. This is exempt from gift tax and no tax return is required for any amount given to a citizen spouse.[7]

---

[4] Internal Revenue Code section 2503(b).
[5] Internal Revenue Code section 2503(e)(2)(A).
[6] Internal Revenue Code section 2503(e)(2)(B).
[7] Internal Revenue Code section 2523(a).

If the spouse receiving the gift is not a United States citizen, no more than $110,000 per year can be given (this amount is indexed and increases each year).[8] If a larger amount is given, it is subject to gift tax.

If the donor is a United States citizen or permanent resident of the United States, then the gift tax exemptions are available to him. Only the citizenship of the spouse-donee is in question and presents a problem if the person is not a citizen.

¶805 Gift Tax Return

If a person makes a gift of over $11,000 in one year to one person or makes a gift of a "future interest," a gift tax return is required.[9] If a gift tax return is due, it must be filed by April 15th of the year following the year of the gift.

If John Doe gives $31,000 to his son on October 15, 2003, he must file a gift tax return by April 15, 2004. The only exception is if the donor dies after making the gift. Because any gift is includable in the estate at death for estate tax purposes, a gift tax return is necessary. Thus, a gift tax return must be filed within nine months of the date of death, or by the following April 15th, whichever is earlier.[10]

If John Doe makes a gift of $31,000 to his son on February 15th but dies on April 1st, the gift tax return would be due within nine months of the date of death, or by January 1st of the following year. If he dies on October 15th, the gift tax return would be due by the following April 15th, because that is earlier than nine months from the date of death.

The gift tax return is Internal Revenue Service form 709. There is no California gift tax return because California does not have a gift tax.

¶806 Gift Tax Rates

The gift tax rates are the same as the estate tax rates. An individual is allowed a lifetime exemption of $1,000,000, so that in most cases no tax is due, but the gift tax return must be filed.

John Doe gives his son $111,000. He is allowed an $11,000 exemption, so the taxable gift is $100,000. A gift tax return is due and the gift tax on $100,000 is $20,800. Because the unified tax credit is $345,800, no tax is due. The return is filed and the gift reported.

For gift tax purposes, all prior taxable gifts are cumulated. If John Doe gave a second $111,000 to his son the following year, he would be making another taxable gift of $100,000, but he has now given away a total of $200,000. Since the tax rates rise, the gift tax is figured on all of the taxable gifts (over $11,000 per donee per year). If the cumulative total exceeds $1,000,000 then a tax is due and must be paid with the return.

---

[8] Internal Revenue Code section 2523(i).
[9] Internal Revenue Code section 6019.
[10] Internal Revenue Code section 6075(b).

Since the government changed the system, the estate and gift tax rates have been combined in a "unified tax system" in effect since late 1976. The advantage of gifting over $11,000 per year has been greatly diminished.

¶807 Gift Splitting Between Spouses

What happens if one spouse has a sizeable amount of separate property and wishes to gift $22,000 of his or her separate property to each of his or her children? Since he or she is giving over $11,000 per donee in one year, a gift tax return is due. Federal law allows, "gift splitting" with a spouse.[11]

This means that a $22,000 gift or a gift of any amount can be treated as if it came equally from husband and wife even though the gift came entirely from the separate property of one spouse. If the total were not more than $22,000 per donee no taxable gift would be made. To gift split, a special federal income tax form, form 709A, is filed and both spouses sign, indicating the gift is treated as coming equally from the two.

¶808 Gifts Made Within Three Years of Death

Formerly, if a person made a gift and died within three years, the value of the gift was included in full in the person's taxable estate. This was changed in 1976. Gifts are not put back into a person's estate unless the donor retained any "strings" on the gift, such as the right to revoke the gift, switch it to another person, or change it.[12]

If a person makes a gift and pays a gift tax, and dies within three years, the tax paid is also put back into the estate. John Doe gives his son $1,111,000. He is allowed an $11,000 gift so that the taxable gift is $1,100,000. Since the gift is over $1,000,000, a gift tax is due. He pays a gift tax of $41,000 ($1,100,000 minus $1,000,000 at 41%). If he dies within three years, the value of the taxable gift ($1,100,000) and the value of the gift tax paid ($41,000) are put back into his estate-a total of $1,141,000. If he dies more than three years after making the gift, only $1,100,000 is put back into his estate. In both cases, he gets a credit for the $41,000 gift tax paid.[13]

The advantage of making large gifts is that the value is determined at the time of the gift. If no "strings" are attached to the gift, that value is used at death. In the prior example, John Doe gave his son real estate with a value of $1,111,000. At his death five years later, the real estate was worth $2,000,000. It was put back into his estate at the gift tax value of $1,100,000, a savings of the tax on $900,000, the increase in value from the date of gift to the date of death.

It can be very beneficial to make gifts of assets that will appreciate from the date of gift to the date of death.

---

[11] Internal Revenue Code section 2513.

[12] Internal Revenue Code sections 2033 and 2035-2038.

[13] Internal Revenue Code section 2035(b).

¶809 Income Tax Basis of Appreciated Assets

While the value of a gift for gift tax purposes is the fair market value as of the date of the gift, what is the income tax basis to the donee that receives the asset? Unfortunately, the basis is not the fair market value. The recipient of the gift steps into the donor's shoes for income tax purposes and does not get a stepped up basis at the time of the gift.

John Doe gives his son $11,000 worth of stock that he purchased for $3,000 a number of years ago. If the stock were kept until John Doe died, it would get a new value at death and if it was worth $11,000 at the father's death, then the son would have a basis for income tax purposes of $11,000. The $8,000 potential capital gains would be forgotten.

However, this is not true with a gift. John Doe's son gets stock worth $11,000, but if he later sells it, he must use his father's cost basis of $3,000. For income tax purposes, assets do not get a new value at the time of a gift.

The rule is that the donee's cost basis is the donor's basis or the current fair market value, whichever is less.[14] If the stock cost the father $12,000 but is worth $11,000 at the time of the gift, the cost basis for the donee is $11,000. If it cost $3,000 but is worth $11,000 at the time of gift, the cost basis to the donee is $3,000.

The general rule is never to give away anything that has gone down in value. It is better to sell it and take a capital loss than to lose the loss by giving it away.

¶810 California Uniform Transfers To Minors Act

California, like most states, has provision for gifts to minors, (people under 18 years of age). While a gift can be made outright to a minor, this would normally trigger a court appointed guardianship. This is far too cumbersome and costly for the amounts involved. A trust could also be used but this requires a trustee, the keeping of detailed records, and the filing of an annual trust tax return. Again, it's too cumbersome and costly.

An alternative is to make a gift under the provisions of the California law known as the *California Uniform Transfers to Minors Act*.[15] Under this act, a custodian manages the assets which can be stock, mutual funds, real estate, cash or any other asset on behalf of the minor, and can invest the assets as the custodian feels is proper. The minor is considered the owner of the assets and the minor's social security number is used. All taxable income is reported to the minor.

The custodian can use the funds for the minor's benefit and when the minor attains age 18, turns the assets over to the minor. If the minor dies, the assets are part of the minor's estate and if he or she dies prior to age 18, the assets pass to the nearest relative by intestate succession.

If it is specified when the gift is made, the assets can be held until age 21. Assets are registered in the name of the custodian, such as "John Doe, Custodian

---

[14] Internal Revenue Code section 1015(a).   [15] California Probate Code sections 3900-3925.

for Frank Doe until age 21, under C.U.T.M.A." If the custodian dies, a new custodian takes over the management. Only one person at a time may serve as custodian.

Although assets may be held until the recipient is age 21, gifts can only be made under the act if the recipient is under age 21. A gift to a 17-year old son can be made and held under the act until he is 21. A gift to an 18-year old son must be made either directly to the boy or under the provisions of this act until he is age 21.

If the custodian is the donor of the gift and dies while acting as custodian, the full value of the assets will be taxed in the donor's estate. To avoid the estate tax, the donor and custodian should be different people. John Doe wants to make a gift to his grandson, who is eight years of age. If John Doe is the custodian and dies while custodian, the gift or gifts will be taxed in his estate. It would be better for John Doe to name his daughter, his grandson's mother, as custodian. If he then dies, none of the assets are taxable in his estate.

¶811 Interest Free Loans

It is not possible to make loans without charging a "reasonable" rate of interest. The government publishes monthly charts setting forth the average interest rate for certain government securities. If a loan is below market rate, that is, the interest is less than that published by the federal government, the lender must report taxable interest at 120% of what the government tables show as the current interest.[16]

The tables are divided into sections for loans of 0-3 years, 3-7 years, and over 7 years. Interest rates vary depending upon whether the interest is paid monthly, quarterly, semi-annually or annually. If the current government table for a 3-year loan with interest paid monthly is 3.14%, the taxpayer will have income tax problems if he or she charges less than this amount.

There are two exceptions to this rule. You can loan $10,000 to any person you wish and as long as the loan does not exceed $10,000, no interest is required.[17] Husband and wife are viewed as one person for loan purposes, so that it is not possible for a couple to loan $40,000 to a son and daughter-in-law. $10,000 is the maximum.

The second exception provides that you can loan a total of $100,000 to someone as long as the borrower's total net investment income for the year does not exceed approximately $1,000.[18] The purpose is to prevent someone in a high income tax bracket from loaning money to a child who is in a lower tax bracket and invests the funds. If the child uses the money to pay off bills, buy a home or purchase other assets, then this will not create a problem. The maximum exception is $100,000. Above that, the government minimum interest rates will apply.

---

[16] Internal Revenue Code section 7872.
[17] Internal Revenue Code section 7872(c)(2).
[18] Internal Revenue Code section 7872(d)(1).

¶812 Qualified Disclaimers

The federal government has allowed people, in some cases, to make gifts without having a gift tax liability. If the nature of the gift is a qualified "disclaimer," then it is not treated as a gift.

Someone who receives an inheritance or gift, whether by beneficiary designation, will, intestate succession, or living trust, may disclaim or refuse the inheritance or gift. If certain requirements are met, it is not treated as a gift and is free of gift tax.

John Doe inherits $100,000 from his mother's estate when she dies. John Doe has a large estate and is making gifts to his children to reduce the estate tax at his death. He would like this $100,000 to go to his children. If he disclaims it and if his mother's will provides it goes to his children, then John Doe's children receive the $100,000 and there is no gift tax involved.

One problem with disclaiming is that a person may not disclaim in favor of someone. One can only refuse the gift or inheritance and then it passes to whoever is entitled to it by law. If John Doe disclaims the $100,000 inheritance, then John Doe is treated as if he died ahead of his mother. His mother's will then controls and if he died ahead of his mother and the will provides his inheritance goes to his children, then his children receive the $100,000. If the will provides the inheritance goes to his brother, then John Doe may not wish to disclaim.

It is possible to disclaim a portion of assets that a person is receiving or a specific asset or assets. It is not necessary to disclaim everything.

Certain requirements are necessary to disclaim assets at death.[19] They include:

1. The disclaimer must be irrevocable and delivered to the executor or person who has the assets that are being disclaimed.

2. The disclaimer must be executed within nine months of the date of death.

3. The disclaimer must be executed before the party disclaiming receives any of the benefits. You cannot disclaim assets after you have received any income or earnings on the assets or after the assets have been distributed to you.

Disclaiming is a good "post mortem" form of estate planning to transfer assets after death and avoid the gift tax on these assets. The disclaiming must be done promptly and in accordance with federal and California law.

Frank Doe and Mary Doe hold all of their assets in their names as community property. Frank Doe dies and his will leaves everything to his wife. The value of the couple's combined estate is over $4,000,000. Since Frank Doe owns one-half of the community property or $2,000,000, Mary Doe may disclaim a portion of the assets, or $1,500,000. This then goes to the children's estate, tax-free. The wife then receives the balance of the assets, or $2,500,000. Although there is no immediate savings, upon Mrs. Doe's later death the estate tax savings

---

[19] Internal Revenue Code section 2518.

will amount to approximately $700,000, because her estate will be only $2,500,000 instead of $4,000,000.

¶813 Irrevocable Trusts and Crummey Provisions

Many people wish to set up a trust for children, grandchildren, or other relatives. They then wish to give up to $11,000 per year per person to the trust. The trust frequently provides that payments may be made for health, support, maintenance, and education, and the beneficiary receives his or her share of the trust assets at age 25, 30, 35, or some other age. The problem is that such a trust does not qualify for the $11,000 per year gift tax exemption.

To qualify for the $11,000 per year gift tax exemption, the gift must be one referred to in the Internal Revenue Code as a gift of a "present interest."[20] A gift of a present interest is one given to the recipient right now without restrictions, or locked up until age 21, subject to certain restrictions. If the gift is "tied" up until after age 21, it is a gift of a "future interest" and does not qualify for the $11,000 per year exemption.[21]

How does one qualify such a trust to allow the $11,000 per year exemption? One way is to place provisions in the trust regarding what is referred to as "Crummey" provisions. These provisions relate to a tax court case in which the petitioner was a taxpayer named Crummey.

"Crummey" provisions allow the beneficiary to revoke the trust and to remove the current gift for a limited period of time, such as 30 days. If the gift is not revoked, then the recipient may not later revoke the trust and remove the gift. By creating a window whereby the beneficiary can remove the $11,000 each year, it will convert the future gift to one of a present gift and then qualify for the annual $11,000 exemption.

John and Mary Doe set up an irrevocable trust for their three children and name a friend as the trustee. Each year they both give $11,000 per child to the trust, or $66,000 per year. After each gift is made, the trustee writes a letter to each child telling the child that he has 30 days to notify the trustee and revoke the gift. If the gift is not revoked within 30 days, then the child's right to later revoke it expires. The trustee can use assets of the trust for each child's health, support, maintenance, and education. Any assets left in the trust go to the child at age 35.

Over a 10-year period the parents can give $66,000 per year, or a total of $660,000 to the trust. The total estate tax savings may be as high as $300,000.

Irrevocable trusts and trusts with Crummey provisions are not for everyone, but work well in certain situations. They are one tool in connection with estate planning.

---

[20] Internal Revenue Code section 2503(b)(i).   [21] Internal Revenue Code section 2503(b)(i).

¶814 Advantages of Making Gifts

Gifts are an excellent way to save estate taxes at death. If the individual has over $1,500,000 to $3,500,000 of assets at death, depending upon the year of death, there will be an estate tax unless assets are left to charitable organizations or a spouse. Gifts of up to $11,000 per person per year will not be put back in the donor's estate unless the donor retains some interest over the gifted property. If a full and completed gift is made, the assets will not be put back in the donor's estate, even if the gifts were made only hours before death.

Gifts of assets of more than $11,000 per year may be worthwhile if the assets are likely to appreciate between the date of gift and date of death. If so, the appreciation will be out of the donor's estate at death. Consideration must be given to income tax cost basis, because the gifted property will not receive a new or stepped up cost basis at death.

Chapter 9

CHARITABLE GIVING

¶900 Introduction

Charitable giving has been a part of American culture for centuries. As government funding declines, charities are needed to take the slack by providing the assistance needed to hold our civilized society together. Each year, more charitable organizations qualify under our tax laws as charitable organizations as people find a need to help treat a disease or support a cause. Some organizations that were formerly nationwide have fragmented into smaller independent organizations. Political groups have formed charitable arms to expand their philosophy and support groups have been organized to support refugees from wars and famines.

¶901 Charitable Gifts

A charitable gift can be a gift of virtually anything. Cash, stock, real estate, vehicles, limited partnerships, furniture, art objects, or other assets may be given to a charitable organization. Giving your time and effort may psychologically be rewarding, but it does not produce any tax deduction.

A check is valid as a gift when given. Credit card charges are good when the credit slip is signed. I.O.U.'s or promises to pay are only deductible when fulfilled or paid.

When you buy a ticket to a charity event, the charitable deduction is only the excess that you pay over the retail value of the ticket.

¶902 Valuation

The value of a gift, for gift tax purposes, is the current fair market value of the asset at the date of gift.[1] If an individual gives a charity 100 shares of stock which is traded at $50 per share on the date of gift, a gift of $5,000 is made. The rules for valuation of charitable gifts are no different than for gifts to individuals.

The valuation of other assets, such as real estate, art objects, furniture, antiques and others are more difficult. Every year, the tax court hears cases where the I.R.S. alleges that the value of the gift to charity is vastly overstated. It is necessary to get a written appraisal of assets other than cash and securities that are regularly traded on a major stock or bond exchange. The appraisal report and a special income tax form must be attached to the tax return on which one claims the deduction.

---

[1] Internal Revenue Code section 2512.

¶903 Income Tax Deduction

One of the reasons people make gifts to charities is to obtain a deduction on their income tax return. When someone makes a gift to a charity, they normally get an income tax deduction for the fair market value of the asset gifted.[2] If someone gives stock worth $5,000, a tax deduction for this $5,000 gift is given. This is true even if the stock costs you $1,000. If the stock were sold, a $4,000 capital gain would occur, and a tax would be paid on this amount. By giving the stock to charity, no capital gain is due, and the full deduction for the current value is given. The charity may then sell the stock, but since the charity is exempt from income tax, no one pays any tax on the gain.

There is a limit on the itemized deduction that can be taken for gifts to charities during the year. To get the deduction, "itemize" the deductions on schedule A of the income tax return (Form 1040) rather than accept the Internal Revenue Service standard deduction of a fixed amount.

The amount deducted for gifts to charities on a tax return is limited. The deduction for cash gifts cannot exceed 50% of the adjusted gross income for that year.[3] "Adjusted gross income" is the total amount of the taxable income minus certain adjustments. If the deduction exceeds 50%, only 50% on that year's return can be taken off, and the excess can carry over as a deduction for the following five years.[4] An individual's adjusted gross income is $60,000, and gives $50,000 cash to charity. The deduction that year is $30,000 (50% of $60,000), but the remaining $20,000 can be deducted on next year's return, and if not used next year can carry over for the following four years.

If someone gives long-term capital gains assets (assets owned by someone for more than one year), one gets a tax deduction for the current value of the asset.[5] However, the maximum one can deduct on a tax return for the year, if giving gifts to a public charity or private foundation, is 30% of ones adjusted gross income.[6]

An individual again has $60,000 of adjusted gross income, and gives $25,000 of stock to the university. One gets a $25,000 deduction but can only take off $18,000 as a result of this gift for the current year (30% of $60,000). The excess ($7,000) will carry over and can be deducted during the next five years.

Real estate, stocks, bonds, mutual funds, and many other securities qualify for this tax treatment.

California allows the same tax deduction for income tax purposes as does the federal government.[7] For federal income tax purposes, the gift of an appreciated asset does not give rise to the alternative minimum tax, which is a concern of some high income taxpayers. California does require that any capital gains be used in the alternative minimum tax computation.[8]

---

[2] Internal Revenue Code section 170(a).
[3] Internal Revenue Code section 170(b)(1)(B)(ii).
[4] Internal Revenue Code section 170(d)(1)(A).
[5] Internal Revenue Code section 170(b)(1)(C).

[6] Internal Revenue Code section 170(b)(1)(C)(i).
[7] California Revenue & Taxation Code section 17201.
[8] California Revenue & Taxation Code sections 17039 and 17062.

¶903

A corporation can also make gifts, but the maximum deduction is 10% of the corporation's taxable income for that year, with a five-year carryover of any excess.[9]

¶904 Gift Tax

Gifts to a qualified charity or charities are not subject to reporting for gift tax purposes. If the gift made to one charity exceeds $11,000 in one year, a federal gift tax return is not due.[10]

¶905 Estate Tax

As previously mentioned, any amount may be left to a charity or charities at death. Any amounts left are exempt from estate tax, without limit.[11] Unfortunately, bequests at death do not produce any income tax deduction.

If an individual makes a gift during lifetime, this reduces the person's taxable estate and also produces an income tax deduction. It is far better to make a gift during a lifetime than to pass assets at death.

¶906 Qualified Charities

To qualify for the various tax benefits, a charity must be a *qualified* charity. This means that it must meet the requirement of the Internal Revenue Code, that it has a letter from the Internal Revenue Service stating that the charity qualifies.

To qualify, the charity must be a corporation, trust, community trust, fund, or foundation organized in the United States, one of its possessions, the District of Columbia, or any state. The organization must be operated exclusively for religious, charitable, scientific, literary or educational purposes, for national or international sports competition, or for the prevention of cruelty to children or animals. A post or organization of war veterans, or a cemetery company owned and operated exclusively for the benefit of members, also qualifies.[12]

¶907 Types of Charitable Gifts

There are a number of different ways of making gifts to charities. This can be done "outright", by making a direct gift of cash, real estate or securities, by use of a charitable remainder trust, by using a pooled income fund, by a bargain sale, or by a number of other methods.

.01 Outright Gift

A charitable deduction is allowed for gifts to a charity. A deduction is allowed for cash given to a charity. A record must be kept and one must have a letter or receipt from the charity acknowledging the gift. The full value of the gift is deductible, subject to the 50% income tax limit.

If an individual gives a traded stock, bond or mutual fund, or real estate that the person has owned for a year or more, an income tax deduction for the full value of the asset is given, not what it originally cost. An appraisal is needed, and if one is giving assets other than traded securities and these assets are worth

---

[9] Internal Revenue Code section 170(b)(2).
[10] Internal Revenue Code section 2503(b).

[11] Internal Revenue Code section 2055(a).
[12] Internal Revenue Code section 170(c)(2).

more than $5,000, a special Internal Revenue Service form (form 8283) must be attached to the income tax return.[13] To transfer assets, one needs to physically transfer the stock or bond certificates, contact the mutual fund, or record a deed to transfer the real property.

The only complication is if the stock is pledged for a loan or money is owed in terms of a mortgage or deed of trust on the real property. If that occurs, the donor must reduce the value of the charitable gift by the amount owed by the donor.[14] Normally it is not a good idea to transfer an asset subject to any loan or indebtedness.

Transferring the ownership to a charity can transfer life insurance. The value of the gift is the value of the insurance policy at the time of the gift. Transferring the policy is done by contacting the insurance company and obtaining an assignment form. This makes the charity the new owner. An income tax deduction is given for the value of the policy and if the premiums continue to be paid, one can get an income tax deduction for future premiums paid.

Art objects, tangible personal property, boats, and automobiles can also be given to a charity. Here, the appraisal is very important. Many people have given away assets and then tried to get these items appraised at a value much higher than they were worth to get a large income tax deduction. The Internal Revenue Service requires that when the deduction exceeds $5,000 and if the charity sells, exchanges, or disposes of the item within two years of receipt, that a report is made of the sale and sales price to the Internal Revenue Service.[15]

If the tangible personal property is for the use and purpose of the charity, a tax deduction is allowed for the full fair market value of the item.[16] Capital gains do not have to be reported. For example, if someone gives a famous painting to an art museum, a full deduction is given.

However, if the gift has no relation to the charitable purpose of the organization, you only get an income tax deduction for the cost basis of the item.[17] It will reduce the tax deduction to give the painting to the Boy Scouts instead of the local art museum.

.02 Charitable Remainder Trusts

It is possible to set up a special charitable trust, receive benefits from the trust, and get an income tax deduction for a portion of the gift.

These types of charitable trusts are referred to, as charitable remainder trusts. The beneficiary gets a payment for lifetime and the charity gets the "remainder," or what is left over when the trust terminates.

The advantages of the trust are that there is an immediate income tax deduction for a portion of the gift. The Internal Revenue Service uses tables that show the value of a charitable deduction for income tax purposes based on the

---

[13] Internal Revenue regulations 1.170A-13(b).
[14] Internal Revenue Code section 170(f)(5).
[15] Internal Revenue Code section 6050L.

[16] Internal Revenue Code section 170(e)(1)(A)(i).
[17] Internal Revenue Code section 170(e)(1)(B)(i).

person's age, the value of the gift, and the amount of payments received. This gift can run from approximately 10-40% of the value of the asset at the time of gift.

Several years ago, the government changed the rules in connection with the valuation of the trust's charitable remainder interest. The value of the charitable remainder portion of the gift at the date the trust is established must now be a minimum of 10%. Prior to this change, there was not a requirement for a minimum value. This means trusts that continue after the death of the individual or couple for relatives such as children, in most cases, no longer qualify. In addition, trusts set up by a single person or husband and wife, for life, will generally not qualify if the individual or couple is rather young (under age 35). This change does not apply to charitable remainder trusts established prior to July 29, 1997.

The second and very important consideration is that the trust is totally income tax exempt including exemption for capital gains purposes. If one transfers an asset that has appreciated to such a trust one gets an income tax deduction based in part on the current value of the asset. The trust can then sell the asset without payment of any capital gains.

A couple in their 70s owns a small apartment building worth $300,000, and yielding approximately $17,000 per year in income. The couple wishes to be rid of the building and is considering selling it, but they need the income. Their cost basis based on 25 years of ownership is approximately $30,000. If they sell the building they will have a capital gain on $270,000 ($300,000 value minus $30,000 cost). The current capital gains tax will be approximately $90,000, leaving them $210,000 to invest. If they invest the $210,000 at a 6% return, their income will be $12,600 per year.

Instead of selling it, they contribute the property to a charitable trust. They elect a 7% variable return, which means that every year the 7% is paid on the then fair market value of the asset or assets. They get an immediate income tax deduction of approximately $100,000 when they establish the trust. The first year they receive $21,000 (7% of $300,000). The charity later sells the property but there is no income tax on the capital gains. Because of the cost of sale, the second year the assets are only worth $250,000. The couple then receives 7% of this amount, or $17,500. In all cases their income is much higher because they do not pay the capital gains tax and they receive a large charitable deduction at the time of the gift.

The disadvantage is when they both die, the trust terminates and the assets belong to the charity. Their children or other relatives will not receive the $300,000 apartment building.

To compensate for this, some people will buy life insurance with their children or an irrevocable trust as the owner and use the income tax savings to pay the premiums. If $300,000 of life insurance were purchased, it would replace the apartment building.

Charitable Remainder Annuity Trust. There are two types of charitable trusts. The first is called a *charitable remainder annuity trusts*.[18] Here, the individual, or husband and wife, receive a fixed amount which does not change during their lifetime. They must elect to receive at least 5% each year and it can be for a higher amount. The higher the amount and the larger the payments, the lower the charitable deduction.

If one puts $200,000 of assets into trust and elect a 6% return, then the couple and the survivor after one's death would receive $12,000 per year for life. At the death of the individual or both husband and wife, the trust will terminate and the assets pass to the charity. The trust is tax exempt and pays no income tax, but the beneficiary or beneficiaries pay tax on the monies they receive to the extent that it is taxable income in the trust.

A charitable remainder annuity trust does not allow additional contributions of assets after it is set up. The payments are fixed and the trust must terminate upon the death of the individual or upon the death of husband and wife.

Charitable Remainder Unitrust. A *charitable remainder unitrust* is a slightly different vehicle.[19] The trust can run for the lifetime of an individual or couple and continue for up to another 20 years after they die. The percentage selected cannot be less than 5% and cannot change, but the payments may vary. The trust is valued annually and the payments for the following 12 months are based on the value.

If a couple puts $200,000 in a charitable remainder unitrust and selects a 6% return, they will receive $12,000 during the first year. On the anniversary date of the establishment of the trust it is valued again, and the payments for the following 12 months are the percentage of this new value. At the end of the first year the trust has increased in value from $200,000 to $220,000. During the second year the couple then receives 6% of $220,000, or $13,200. This type of trust is like a variable annuity in that the payments change yearly based on the value of the assets.

It is also possible to make additional contributions of assets to a charitable remainder unitrust (but not an annuity trust).[20] If someone wishes to contribute additional assets, a new trust does not have to be established if the donor is happy with the terms of the existing trust.

Although the charities must be designated when the trust is established, the donor can make a provision in the trust to change the charities as long as a charity which is qualified under tax law receives the assets when the trust terminates.[21] While many charities will act as trustees of these types of trust, an individual and even the donor or donors of the trust may be the trustees.

.03 Charitable Lead Trust

The reverse of a charitable remainder trust is a charitable lead trust.[22] This type of trust is used for an entirely different purpose.

---

[18] Internal Revenue Code section 664(d)(1).
[19] Internal Revenue Code section 664(d)(2).
[20] Internal Revenue Code section 664(d)(4).

[21] Internal Revenue Code section 664(d)(2)(C).
[22] Internal Revenue Code section 642(c).

An individual dies with a taxable estate of $10,000,000. The estate tax is approximately $5,000,000. To reduce this tax, the assets stay in trust for a specified number of years with the income from the assets being paid to a designated charity or charities. Based on tax tables, this $10,000,000 estate is reduced by the actuarial value of the period of time and value of the trust. If the trust lasts 15 years and pays out 7% annually, the estate tax may be cut by $1,000,000 or more. The larger the annual payout and the longer the term of years for the charity, the smaller the amount that is left to be taxed.

The disadvantage is that the estate beneficiaries such as the children do not receive the assets for a number of years.

This type of trust only normally works for large estates and works where the estate beneficiaries can afford to part with the assets for a lengthy period of time.

.04 Pooled Income Fund

For someone who wishes an annuity for life, a pooled income fund may be the best vehicle. A pooled income fund is like a charitable mutual fund. An individual contributes cash or marketable securities to the fund. There is no capital gains tax on the assets transferred. The beneficiary receives a charitable deduction based on his or her age, the amount of the gift, and the past earnings of the fund (highest rate of return earned by the fund in the three years prior to gift).

The beneficiary then receives his or her proportionate share of the earnings on the fund while he or she is alive.[23] At his or her death, the fund keeps the income on that share for the charity. Although there is no capital gain, the beneficiary is taxable on monies paid out by the fund each year. Depending upon the person's age, the annual return may be 8%, 9% or 10%.

.05 Personal Residence Trust

A person may transfer his or her home or farm to a charity retaining a "life estate," the right to continue to use and live on the property until death.[24] A personal residence may include not only a personal residence but a vacation home, condo, etc. A ranch may only contain the home and a few surrounding acres.

The person who contributes the property receives an income tax deduction for the value of the property minus his or her lifetime use. This value is based on the property's value and the person's age. At the person's death, the property passes to the charity and is not included in the person's estate for estate tax purposes.

A widow age 65 deeds her home worth $200,000 to a charity retaining the right to use it for her lifetime. Based on the Internal Revenue Service tables, her income tax deduction in the year of gift would be approximately $50,000-60,000.

The individual gets the use of the property for his or her lifetime but cannot sell it since it passes to charity at death. The property can be rented while the individual is alive and the donor receives the income from the rent. The donor

---

[23] Internal Revenue Code section 642(c)(3).   [24] Internal Revenue Code section 170(f)(3)(B).

must keep up the property for his or her lifetime and pay real estate taxes, insurance, and all other maintenance costs.

.06 Bargain Sale

A bargain sale is where property is sold to the charity for a price less than fair market value.[25] The difference between the sales price and the fair market value is the charitable gift, and the individual gets an income tax deduction for this amount.

John Doe sells his property that is appraised for $100,000 to a charity for $60,000. He is making a charitable gift at the time of sale for $40,000.

Unfortunately, the donor does not normally escape tax-free. The person must report the sale and use his or her proportionate share of the cost. In the above example, if the cost of the real estate for income tax purposes is $40,000, and he is selling it for 60% of its value, he only gets 60% of his cost basis. Thus, his cost is $24,000 (60% of $40,000), and the gain if he sells it for $60,000 is the difference, or $36,000. This gain is taxable.

A bargain sale is useful if a person wants some money from the transfer of the asset but wishes a portion to go to the charity.

.07 Scenic Easement

If a person owns real estate and wishes to restrict its future use to a scientific or conservation purpose, the person can give an easement which restricts the future use of the property.[26] Someone may wish to donate land so that it may be a state or local park, and cannot later be sold for home development.

The donor who gives the easement gets an income tax deduction for the reduced value of the land. If it was worth $20,000 per acre for land development and is worth only $5,000 per acre for a park, the $15,000 per acre difference would be an income tax deduction at the time the easement is recorded.

A scenic easement is available for the preservation of land for outdoor recreation; education of the general public; the protection of the natural habitat for fish, wildlife, or plants or similar ecosystem; preservation of open space for the scenic enjoyment of the general public or pursuant to government conservation policies; and for historic structures in the national register or located in a registered historic district.

If a person is interested in such an easement, they should contact one of the local or national organizations, such as The Nature Conservancy, or other similar organizations.

.08 Gift Annuity

A gift annuity is an annuity that pays a fixed amount to a person for his or her lifetime or to a husband and wife for their joint lifetimes. The approximate annual rate of return on the annuity amount based on the person or younger person's age for 2003 is:

---

[25] Internal Revenue Code section 1011(b).   [26] Internal Revenue Code section 170(h).

¶907.06

Age 55	5.50%
60	5.7
65	6.0
70	6.5
75	7.1
80	8.0

A person gives $100,000 to a qualified charity in return for a gift annuity. He or she is age 65 at the time of gift. He or she receives $6,000 per year for the rest of their life. At his or her death the annuity terminates and all funds are kept by the charity. He or she gets an income tax deduction when the annuity is established.

A portion of each annuity payment is tax free for income tax purposes. If the person lives beyond his or her life expectancy then the annuity payments become fully taxable. A person can establish a gift annuity but have the payments start in the future instead of immediately. The charitable income tax deduction is obtained when the annuity is established regardless of when the payments commence.[27]

A widow age 70 gives $25,000 to a charity. She receives annual annuity payments of $1,625 and she gets an income tax deduction when she establishes the gift annuity of approximately $11,000.

Gift annuities are not normally subject to the laws that apply to insurance and annuity companies. The person must rely on the charity for the payments.

¶908 Summary

Charitable giving is important and provides an income tax deduction for the donor, depending upon the type of gift and value. This chapter only presents a very short summary of the opportunities available. There are numerous variations that people may use.

If a person is interested in making such a gift, usually the charity should be contacted directly to discuss the gift and the nature of the gift (trust, outright gift, etc.). An individual should also consult with his or her attorney and accountant before formalizing and completing the gift.

---

[27] Internal Revenue Code section 170(f)(2)(B).

Chapter 10

TRUSTS

¶1000 Introduction

Trusts are probably the most widely used form of estate planning after wills. Many couples and single individuals have a trust drafted to avoid probate, to save estate taxes, to avoid problems upon incapacity, and to take care of special needs for children, grandchildren, or other relatives.

¶1001 Definition of a Trust

A trust is a legal arrangement whereby assets are transferred to someone to hold for another person or people under definite terms and conditions.[1] For instance, a father turns assets over to his brother to hold for his son, with the assets going to the son at age 21. Although trusts can be oral or in writing, this chapter only covers written trusts. The person who manages the trust is defined as the "trustee."[2] A person or people who can receive benefits from the trust are called trust "beneficiaries."[3] At some point, the trust must terminate and go to an individual, individuals, or charity. The people or organizations that ultimately receive the trust assets when the trust terminates are called trust "remainder persons."

Trusts have been around for hundreds of years but have become very popular in the last few decades because they save a large amount of estate taxes for a husband and wife, and they also avoid the probate process for a couple or individual.

Many people set up a trust to take care of someone such as a child. The assets may be used for the child's benefit and go to the child at a certain age or ages, such as one-half at age 30 and the balance at age 35. Or, a trust may continue for a lifetime to take care of someone financially if they are unable to manage the assets and would likely spend the inheritance in a few years.

¶1002 Advantages of a Trust

As has been mentioned, trusts have a number of advantages. *First*, a trust can save estate taxes for husband and wife. Husband and wife each have an estate tax exemption of $1,500,000 to $3,500,000, depending on the year of death. Together, they can shelter $3,000,000 to $7,000,000 from estate tax.

If a husband and wife have $3,000,000 and the husband leaves everything to the wife at his death, there is no estate tax. However, at the wife's later death, she now has $3,000,000, and the federal estate tax would amount to approximately $730,000.

---

[1] California Probate Code section 82.
[2] California Probate Code section 84.
[3] California Probate Code section 24.

If the husband and wife set up a trust, at the husband's death, his half of the assets or $1,500,000 is placed in an irrevocable trust. The wife can be the trustee, receive all of the earnings from the trust, and use the principal of the trust, if needed, for her health, support, and maintenance. This $1,500,000 is taxed when the husband dies but because not more than $1,500,000 is in trust, no tax is due. When the wife later dies, the husband's irrevocable trust is not taxable because the wife is not considered the owner. The wife's half of the assets of $1,500,000 is taxable when she dies, but because she has a $1,500,000 exemption, no tax is due. At the wife's later death, no estate tax is payable, and the savings to the children or others are approximately $730,000.

Second, a living trust avoids the probate process. Mary Doe, a widow, has $500,000 of assets. If she leaves these assets in her name alone, at her death, they will go through probate. The statutory probate fee in California for $500,000 is $13,000 for the executor and $13,000 for the attorney, for a total of $26,000.

Mary Doe can put the assets into joint tenancy with her four children. But, by doing so, she is making a gift and creating a possible problem if she wishes to sell any of the assets or if the children have financial problems.

Mary Doe can set up a revocable living trust in which she is the initial trustee. She can do anything she wishes with the trust while she is alive. At death, her daughter becomes the successor trustee. The daughter, as trustee, sells assets, pays bills and taxes, and distributes the assets to the four children. No probate is necessary. An attorney may be consulted for advice, but the fee charged would be a small portion of what the probate fee would have been.

Third, a trust can financially "take care" of someone. John and Mary Smith have a mentally retarded son who requires a great deal of care. If money is left to the child, he will be unable to legally manage it. Instead, it is left in trust for his lifetime so that he can be financially taken care of without the need for a court ordered conservatorship.

Grandparents wish to set up a trust to provide for their grandchildren for college. At the death of both grandparents, $200,000 is set-aside in a separate trust to pay for college and related expenses of the grandchildren. After the last grandchild completes college or attains a certain age, the trust terminates and the assets pass either to the grandchildren, who can use the funds for home or investment, or go to the couple's children.

Trusts can also be used to delay distribution if the beneficiary is too young to receive the assets. Parents die with minor children. Without a trust, the assets go into a guardianship and go to the children at age 18. It is far better to set up a trust so that $500,000 is set aside and used financially for the children, with each child receiving one-half of his or her share at age 25, and the balance at age 30. Presumably the child will be more mature at those ages than at age 18.

Fourth, a trust can be used as a vehicle to manage assets. Although a couple's only child seems financially responsible, she will inherit $3,000,000 after estate taxes. The parents leave it in trust so the daughter receives the income and principal if she needs it for her lifetime. It is professionally managed by a bank trust department and she receives $120,000 per year income from the trust.

¶1002

Fifth and last, a living trust can avoid the legal problems when someone becomes incapacitated. If Mary Doe has all of her assets in her name alone and has not given someone a power of attorney, upon her incapacity and inability to manage her assets, a court appointed conservator would be needed. If Mary Doe sets up a living trust and transfers her assets to the trust, then upon her incapacity, even if she is the trustee, the next named trustee will take over the management of the trust. It will not be necessary to go through an involved and costly legal process.

¶1003 Types of Trusts

Trusts can be divided using two different criteria. First, there are living trusts and testamentary trusts. Second, trust can be divided between revocable and irrevocable trusts.

.01 Living Trust

A *living trust* is a trust established while a person is alive. A written document called a trust agreement or trust declaration is prepared and signed by the person or couple.[4] A trust can be established by an individual or by husband and wife. It takes effect immediately and trust assets are transferred to the trust.

With a living trust it is necessary to register assets in the name of the trustee of the trust. Assets might be registered in the name of "Mary Doe, Trustee of the Mary Doe Living Trust, dated 4-11-2003." Upon the death of Mary Doe or upon her incapacity, the next named trustee, such as her niece, takes over the management of the trust as the trustee.

A living trust avoids probate, whether for an individual or couple, saves estate taxes for a husband and wife, and avoids legal problems upon incapacity.

With a single person there is one trust. At the death of the trust creator, the trust can terminate and the assets can be distributed, or the trust can continue on in whole or in part for the benefit of certain people. Mary Doe provides that at her death the trust is divided into equal shares for her four children. Three children receive their shares outright, but one daughter's share stays in trust for her lifetime, going to the daughter's children when the daughter dies.

With a husband and wife, the living trust in a community property state such as California is handled by having one single trust jointly executed by the couple. Assets, such as community property assets, are transferred into the trustee's name and remain community property.[5] Any separate property assets of either spouse can be transferred into the trust and remains as separate property of that spouse.[6] The trust continues as a revocable trust. The couple can buy and sell assets, and no separate income tax return is required for the trust as long as either husband or wife, or both, are the trustees. Income in terms of interest, dividends, and capital gains is reported on the couple's personal income tax return. There is no taxation for transferring assets into the trust, and there is no reassessment of California real estate by such a transfer.[7]

---

[4] California Probate Code section 15200.
[5] California Family Code section 761.

[6] California Family Code section 770.
[7] California Revenue & Taxation Code section 621(d).

At the death of either husband or wife, the trust is divided into two sub-trusts, that are frequently called "Trust A" and "Trust B." Sometimes different titles are used, such as "exemption trust," "survivor's trust," "family trust," or some other term.

Trust B contains the decedent's assets. This would hold the decedent's separate property and his or her one-half of the couple's community property. This amount cannot exceed the estate tax exemption in the year of death, if it does, the excess is usually added to the survivor's trust; trust A. Trust B becomes an irrevocable trust at the first death. Normally, the surviving spouse is the sole trustee. The survivor generally receives all of the income or earnings from the trust and the surviving spouse can receive principal if he or she needs it for health, support, or maintenance.

At the surviving spouse's death, Trust B may terminate and go to the couple's children, or may go to others, or may continue in trust, depending upon the terms of the trust. There are no taxes on Trust B upon the surviving spouse's death and no probate at either death.

Trust A continues as a revocable trust for the surviving spouse. Trust A contains the survivor's separate property, the survivor's half of the couple's community property, and the excess of the decedent's assets if the total is over $1,500,000 to $3,500,000, depending on the year of death. If a couple has $2,000,000 of community property and one spouse dies in 2004, Trust A and Trust B will each have $1,000,000 of assets. If the couple has $4,000,000 of assets, only a maximum of $1,500,000 may go to Trust B, and the remainder, or $2,500,000, will go to Trust A.

The surviving spouse can revoke, amend, or change Trust A. At the survivor's death, if Trust A has not been changed, after payment of taxes and debts, the assets normally follow the disposition of Trust B. There will be no probate of the assets in Trust A at either death, but at the death of the surviving spouse, Trust A will be taxable for federal estate tax purposes with a $1,500,000 to $3,500,000 exemption, depending on the year of death. If the assets in Trust A and the assets owned by the surviving spouse outside the trust exceed the exemption amount, an estate tax will have to be paid within nine months of the survivor's death.

Pour-over Will. Even though an individual or a couple have a living trust, there frequently are still assets in the person's name at death. This may include an automobile, furniture, bank account or accounts, or other assets. If the assets are in joint tenancy, they pass to the surviving joint tenant. If the assets are in the decedent's name alone, they are picked up by his or her will.

Most people who have a living trust also have what is referred to as a "pour-over" will. The will leaves furniture, automobiles, and personal items to the spouse, if there is one, and if not, to the children equally. Any other assets that are picked up by the will are added to or "pour-over" to the living trust, to follow the disposition of the trust. If the value of the assets at death, excluding

¶1003.01

any automobiles, does not exceed $100,000, no probate will be necessary.[8] If they exceed $100,000, then probate will be required. In any case, the assets will be added to the living trust. If a person or couple wishes to amend or change the living trust, they do not have to change the will because the living trust controls the disposition of assets at death.

.02 Testamentary Trust

A *testamentary trust* is one that is established in a person's will. The trust comes into being at the time of the person's death. Unfortunately, in order to get the assets into the trust, they must first go through the probate process. A testamentary trust can save taxes for husband and wife similar to a living trust. However, it does not avoid probate and does not prevent a conservatorship if the party becomes incapacitated before death.

At the person's death, the assets go through the probate process. At the conclusion of probate, the assets are distributed to the designated trustee, who holds the assets subject to the terms of the trust which are set forth, in detail, in the will. If the person who dies is married, two trusts can be set up-Trust A and Trust B. Here, only the decedent's half of the couple's community property and the decedent's separate property are subject to probate. The surviving spouse keeps his or her half of the community property and his or her own separate property apart from these trusts.

If the couple has $2,000,000 of community property, one-half, or $1,000,000 is probated and goes into an irrevocable trust tax-free. The surviving spouse would keep his or her $1,000,000, which would go through probate at his or her death.

Testamentary trusts are not used on a regular basis. Normally, if a husband and wife want a trust to save taxes and avoid probate, they will use a living trust. If a single person wants to avoid probate, a living trust is used.

A testamentary trust may be used in the unlikely event both husband and wife die prior to the children reaching a certain age, say age 30. If both husband and wife die, they may wish their assets held in trust and used for the children, with each child getting his or her share at age 30. The chances of both spouses dying are remote, so a simple testamentary trust may be used.

.03 Revocable Trusts

Most living trusts which are set up are revocable until death.[9] If a couple or a single person sets up a revocable trust, they wish to be able to control the trust, possibly making changes in it, and handle it any way they wish. The trust remains revocable until death.

At death, the trust may terminate or continue. If it continues, the person does not wish the beneficiary to have the right to revoke the trust, so it becomes irrevocable.

With a husband and wife, their trust is normally revocable until the first spouse dies. Then Trust B becomes an irrevocable trust while Trust A stays as a

---

[8] California Probate Code sections 13050 and 13100.   [9] California Probate Code section 15400.

revocable trust. If Trust B were revocable by the surviving spouse, then the surviving spouse legally would own the assets and all of the assets would be taxed at death. The tax savings would be nullified.

If a person drafts a testamentary trust, the will is revocable until death, so the trust stays revocable until the testator dies.

.04 Irrevocable Trusts

Most trusts become irrevocable at death. If they do not, then the person who can revoke the trust can change it, and the assets are taxable at death. If a person wishes a trust to continue for a son's lifetime, one normally wants it to be irrevocable since one does not wish the son to be able to revoke or cancel the trust.

It is possible to set up an irrevocable trust during a person's lifetime (before death) for someone's benefit. Here, the rules become complex. If a person sets up an irrevocable trust and places assets in the trust, one will be taxed on these assets when they die if they are the trustee, if they have the right to income or principal payments from the trust, or if they retain any interest in the trust.[10] A person cannot set up an irrevocable trust, place assets in the trust, receive the income from the trust for life, and not have the assets taxed when they die.

A person can set up an irrevocable trust for children or grandchildren as long as someone else is the trustee. The trust is irrevocable and one does not receive any benefits or interest in the trust in the future. Very few people wish to do this. In addition, to make gifts to such a trust it may be necessary to put in "crummey" provisions to qualify for the gift tax exemption (see Chapter 8).

¶1004 Parties To a Trust

There are a number of different parties or people involved in a trust. The *"trustor," "grantor,"* or *"settlor"* is the person or couple who set up or establish the trust. That person or persons will not change. The John Doe and Mary Doe living trust will continue under that name even after the people die.

The *"trustee"* or *"trustees"* are the managers of the trust, will vary. Husband and wife usually are the co-trustees of their own trust. At the first death, the surviving spouse becomes the sole trustee of both Trust A and Trust B. After the surviving spouse dies, their three children become the successor co-trustees.

The named trustee or trustees continue until death, resignation, or incapacity. Most trust documents provide that "incapacity" is defined as a written statement, signed by two physicians, that the trustee is, in their opinion, unable to function as the trustee. The next named trustee or trustees can then take over the management of the trust by obtaining a death certificate, resignation, or written letter signed by two doctors regarding incapacity.

The *"beneficiary"* is the person or persons who have the right to currently receive payments from the trust. These payments may be fixed, such as all of the income or earnings from the trust, or it may be discretionary, based on need.

---

[10] Internal Revenue Code sections 2033 and 2036-2038.

The *"contingent beneficiary"* is the people who receive payments from the trust in the future. A husband dies and sets up a trust for his wife. She is the current beneficiary. At the wife's death, the trust continues for the children's lifetime and each child receives income from his or her trust. The children then become beneficiaries at their mother's death.

The *"remainder persons"* are the people who receive the trust when the trust terminates. A trust cannot run forever, and when it terminates it must go to designated parties. A trust runs for the wife's lifetime and at her death it terminates and goes to the couple's three children. The three children are the "remainder persons."

¶1005 Terms of Trust

A trust must specifically state what happens in terms of payments. Nothing is automatic or implied.

A revocable trust allows the creator of the trust to do anything he or she wishes.

An irrevocable trust, or a revocable trust that becomes irrevocable, must state specifically what payments are made and who may receive payments.

Income is defined as what a trust earns in terms of interest, dividends and net rents.[11] It does not normally include capital gains.[12] Most trusts provide that all of the income is paid to the trust beneficiary or beneficiaries. It is then taxed to these parties and not to the trust. The current trust income tax rates are high, with net income (after expenses) subject to a top tax rate of 38.6% on income over $9,200.

Some trusts give the trustee the discretion to pay out the income to various people (what is termed "sprinkle" it). If it is paid out it is taxed to the party and, if it is retained in the trust, it is taxed to the trust.

Most trusts provide that payments may also be made from the principal or corpus of the trust. These payments are normally not taxable. Payments can be made for any reason but usually the payments are only allowed for "health, support, maintenance, and education." These four terms are ascertainable standards in that any person may be the trustee and determine payments to the beneficiary without tax problems. Mary Doe is trustee of her husband's trust. She receives all of the income and she can take out principal if she needs it for health, support, and maintenance. Even though she can use principal, the assets in the trust are not taxable at her death because these powers are permissible.[13]

If the terms are too broad, such as "joy, welfare, comfort, happiness," these will create a tax problem. If Mary Doe can take money out of principal of her husband's irrevocable trust for her "comfort," she will be taxable on all of the trust assets at her death.[14]

A trust should provide what happens to the income and if principal payments can be made from the trust. If nothing is said, payments cannot be made.

---

[11] California Probate Code section 16324.

[12] California Probate Code sections 16324 and 16350.

[13] Internal Revenue Code section 2041(b)(1)(A).

[14] Internal Revenue regulation 20.2041-1.

The wife may receive all of the income from the trust and payments can be made for the wife, children, and grandchildren from principal for health, support, maintenance, and education.

Some people provide that a monthly annuity or fixed amount is paid from the trust that is not changeable. Other trusts provide that the income is accumulated, taxed, and added to principal for some period of time, and is then distributed.

It is also possible to give someone the right to withdraw up to a certain amount from the trust each year without creating tax problems. The maximum that a person can withdraw each year is 5% of the value of the trust at the end of the year, or $5,000, whichever is greater.[15]

Mary Doe receives all of the income from her husband's trust. She can withdraw 5% or $5,000 per year if the trust states that she can. At the end of the year, the trust is worth $300,000. She can then withdraw $15,000. If she fails to spend this amount, she only increases her estate by $15,000 for estate tax purposes and takes $15,000 out of assets that would go estate tax free to other people.

The other concern is who shall act as the trustee. If the trust becomes irrevocable, the provision as to who shall be the trustee or trustees cannot be changed.

Anyone can serve as trustee. An individual can be named, or several people can serve jointly as co-trustees.[16] A California bank or trust company can serve if the trust is large enough.[17] Most major banks will not take a trust that is less than $1,000,000 in value. If there are two trusts, each should be over the minimum amount. Some smaller banks or trust companies will take a trust if it has a value of at least $500,000.

The trustee or trustees must carry out the legal duties of a trustee.[18] This includes carrying out the terms of the trust such as investing trust assets, keeping detailed records, making the required payments, and filing the annual income tax returns. The trustee must have sufficient time and the maturity or experience to know what has to be done, or must be able to obtain information from a professional, such as an attorney.

¶1006 Trust Investments

The trustee has the responsibility to invest the funds and assets of the trust, subject to any restrictions in the will, trust agreement, or trust declaration.[19] Trust investments normally must be "prudent" investments.[20] That is, they must be reasonable at the time they are made.

The trustee has a legal obligation to monitor investments and to diversify these investments so that not all investments are in a single security. The trustee must also balance the difference between the current income, which goes to the

---

[15] Internal Revenue Code section 2041(b)(2)(B).
[16] California Probate Code section 15620.
[17] California Probate Code section 83.

[18] California Probate Code sections 16000-16015.
[19] California Probate Code sections 16220-16249.
[20] California Probate Code section 16040.

income beneficiary, and the appreciation, which goes to the trust remainder persons.

If an individual serves as trustee, that individual normally seeks help in terms of having a financial planner, broker, or other professional advise them as to the investments.

If the trust document directs the trustee as to what investments can be made, the trustee must follow such direction.

¶1007 Taxation of Trusts

The taxation of trusts is complicated. If a trust is revocable, all income and taxable gains are taxed yearly to the trustor or creator of the trust. For estate tax purposes, the trustor owns the trust assets and at death, all of these assets are subject to estate tax.

An irrevocable trust is taxed differently. If the income is to be paid directly out, then the income is taxed to the trust beneficiary and not to the trust. If the income may be legally accumulated or paid out, it is taxed to the trust if accumulated and it is taxed to the beneficiary if paid out. If it is required that the income be accumulated, it is taxed to the trust. Any capital gains are normally taxed to the trust.

For estate tax purposes if a trust is irrevocable and was not created by the beneficiary, it will normally not be taxed when the beneficiary dies. If John Doe dies and sets up an irrevocable trust for his wife, the trust assets are generally taxed when the husband dies and are not taxed at the wife's death. The exception is a qualified terminable interest trust described below.

¶1008 Generation-Skipping Trust

A generation-skipping trust is an irrevocable trust that continues for the lifetime of at least one generation, (mentioned in chapter 7).

John Doe dies and sets up an irrevocable trust for his wife. After her death, the irrevocable trust continues for the lifetime of the children, and as each child dies, that share passes to the deceased child's children. This is termed a generation-skipping trust because it continues for a child's lifetime and goes to grandchildren thus, it skips a generation.

Because the trust is irrevocable, it is not taxed in the child's estate. Because it escapes estate tax, the government has created another applicable tax called a "generation-skipping transfer tax."

The generation-skipping tax is imposed for irrevocable trusts created after October 22, 1986. Trusts that became irrevocable before that date are exempt and not subject to tax.[21] The generation-skipping tax is imposed on the assets based on their value when the next generation dies, such as the death of a child. There is a $1,500,000 to $3,500,000 exemption per decedent depending on the year of death, based on the assets which go into trust.[22] The excess is then taxed at the

---

[21] Internal Revenue Code section 2601.   [22] Internal Revenue Code section 2631.

highest estate tax rate in effect when the next generation inherits (currently 45-48%).[23]

John Doe dies in 2004 and sets up an irrevocable trust for the lifetime of his son. At the time of his death the assets are valued at $2,000,000. Since the exemption is $1,500,000, 75% of the trust is exempt. When the son dies, the trust has grown to $4,000,000. 75% is exempt and 25% is taxable, so $1,000,000 is subject to the generation skipping tax. The current tax rate is 48% so that the generation-skipping tax is $480,000 (48% of $1,000,000). The balance of the trust is not subject to any other tax.

If a person sets up a trust that will skip a generation, it is important to plan the $1,500,000 to $3,500,000 exemption for the decedent for both husband and wife to fully utilize this and save taxes.

¶1009 Qualified Terminable Interest Trust

A qualified terminable interest trust is a special type of irrevocable trust for the benefit of a person's spouse.[24]

John Doe dies and he and his wife have community property of $2,000,000. His half is $1,000,000. The estate tax exemption is $1,500,000, so he sets this amount aside in a special exemption trust called Trust B. He has an excess of $500,000. What does he do with this amount?

If this $500,000 is just left in trust, it is taxable and will generate a tax of approximately $225,000. If it is given to the surviving spouse, either outright or in the survivor's revocable trust, it is not taxable since the surviving spouse is exempt. However, the surviving spouse then owns the assets and can leave these assets to anyone she wishes at death. If this is the couple's second marriage and each has children from a former marriage who they wish to inherit their assets, problems may arise. If the wife inherits this $500,000, she may leave it, at death, to her children and not to the husband's children.

To exercise control over these assets, the husband can set up a second irrevocable trust at death called a qualified terminable interest trust. This is an irrevocable trust only for the spouse's benefit. The surviving spouse receives all of the income or earnings from the trust. The surviving spouse may or may not receive principal in the event of need. No other person may receive payments from the trust during the surviving spouse's lifetime.[25] At the surviving spouse's death, the assets go to whomever the husband directed, not to the wife's children.

John Doe places the $500,000 in a qualified terminable interest trust. His wife receives the income for life and at her death, it goes to his children and she can exercise no control over the assets at death.

For estate tax purposes, the assets are not taxed at the first death but are taxed when the surviving spouse dies. At the wife's death, the assets would be added to the value of all other assets that she owned and the estate tax imposed.

---

[23] Internal Revenue Code section 2641.
[24] Internal Revenue Code section 2056(b)(7).
[25] Internal Revenue Code section 2056(b)(7)(B)(ii).

The taxes on the trust assets are paid out of the trust and not by the spouse's relatives.

A qualified terminable interest trust is used where control of the assets is important. If a couple who has been married for 50 years sets up a trust, this type of trust may not be needed. However, if John Doe remarries and has $2,000,000 of separate property assets, he may wish his wife to be taken care of financially but not wish her to be able to leave the assets to her relatives at death. A qualified terminable interest trust for the excess $500,000 would be useful to be sure these assets go to his children at his wife's later death.

The estate taxes are unchanged, whether the assets go directly to the spouse or into a qualified terminable interest trust for the spouse's benefit.

¶1010 Qualified Domestic Trust

In 1988, Congress elected to change the estate tax law to correct what was deemed a problem, leaving assets at death to a non-citizen spouse. The estate tax law provided that if the decedent was married at death, he or she could leave assets to the surviving spouse, estate tax free. If the surviving spouse was not a United States citizen, then the spouse could return to his or her country of origin and the assets would not be taxed by the United States at death.

This was changed for individuals dying after November, 1988. In order for the marital deduction to apply and tax not to be due, a special type of trust called a "qualified domestic trust" must be used or estate tax paid at death.[26]

In many cases this type of trust is not necessary. If John Doe dies and has assets of not more than $1,500,000 to $3,500,000, depending on the year of death, the estate tax exemption will cover this amount and it will not be a problem. It is only when the decedent's assets are over the estate tax exemption that there is a problem. California community property laws will apply so that a couple who has resided in California for a lengthy period of time may have up to $3,000,000 of community property, giving the decedent not more than $1,500,000. The citizenship of the decedent is not a problem, only the citizenship of the surviving spouse.

If the decedent dies with assets of over $1,500,000 or more and the surviving spouse is not a United States citizen (residency does not matter), then the only way to avoid paying tax is to set up a qualified domestic trust or to have the spouse become a United States citizen before the estate tax return is filed.[27]

This qualified domestic trust can be set up after death by the surviving spouse.[28] If that is done, it has to be an irrevocable trust which may create some gift tax and income tax problems.

If the decedent has $3,000,000 when he dies, he can use his $1,500,000 exemption to set up a standard exemption trust, Trust B. The excess of $500,000 can be placed in a special qualified domestic trust for his wife. This is an irrevocable trust for the sole benefit of the spouse. The spouse gets all of the

[26] Internal Revenue Code section 2056A.
[27] Internal Revenue Code section 2056A(b)(12).
[28] Internal Revenue Code section 2056(e).

income or earnings from the trust. Principal can be used if the spouse needs it but it is subject to estate tax. Mary Doe later gets a $10,000 payment from her deceased husband's qualified domestic trust. A supplemental estate tax must be filed and the estate tax paid on this $10,000, just as if the decedent had been taxed on $1,510,000 at death.[29]

The trustee or co-trustee of this trust must be a United States citizen, and the trust assets must remain in the United States.[30] Several other technical rules apply.

When the surviving spouse dies, the assets in the trust are treated as the spouse's assets and taxed with the spouse's assets.

When a spouse or both husband and wife are not citizens of the United States and either spouse will have more than $1,500,000 at death, consideration must be given to the use of this type of trust. The only alternative is to have the spouse become a United States citizen before the estate tax return is filed.

¶1011 California Trust Law

California has a provision that is loosely called, trust law-probate code sections 15000 and following. This allows the Superior Court to review actions the trustee has taken, require an accounting by the trustee, replace a trustee where none is named in the document, or any other legal action with regard to trusts.

The law sets up a procedure for the court to get the trustee into court and to interpret the trust or take whatever legal action is necessary.[31] Normally, trusts do not get involved with the courts and this procedure is rarely used.

When a trust becomes irrevocable due to a person's death, the trustee must mail a specifically worded notice to all persons named in the trust and all of the decedent's heirs at law within 60 days of the date of death. Each party must be advised that he or she has 120 days from the date of mailing to contest the trust. If a person is mailed notice and does not contest the trust within the 120-day period, they cannot later contest it.

If notice is not mailed to a required party, that party may contest the trust many years later.

In connection with a living trust for husband and wife, when the first spouse dies notice must be given to "everyone" who may have an interest in the trust. Since the trust does not usually terminate until the death of the second spouse, this notice must cover everyone who may inherit. Depending upon the wording in the trust it may cover children, grandchildren, great grandchildren, and even other relatives or charities. Also, notice must be given to all "heirs at law," who are the people who would receive the decedent's assets if he or she died without a will. Any of the parties receiving notice can request and receive a copy of the living trust agreement or declaration and all amendments made to it before death.

---

[29] Internal Revenue Code section 2056A(b)(5)(A).   [31] California Probate Code sections 17000-17211.
[30] Internal Revenue Code section 2056A(a)(1)(A).

Upon the death of the surviving spouse, notice again must be sent out to all parties who inherit the surviving spouse's portion of the trust and all of the surviving spouse's heirs at law.

For an unmarried person, this notice must be sent to all required parties when the trustor dies.

¶1012 Dynasty Trusts

During the last few years, with the large increase in the federal estate tax exemption and the generation-skipping transfer tax exemption, many couples have been establishing long term generation-skipping trusts, referred to as "dynasty trusts."

These are basically living trusts that continue after the death of husband and wife for several generations. Starting in 2004, the estate tax and generation-skipping transfer tax exemption per decedent is $1,500,000, rising to $2,000,000 in 2006, and is scheduled to increase in the future.

A husband and wife have $4,000,000 in total assets and have established a standard A-B living trust. The husband dies in 2006 and $2,000,000 goes into Trust B tax exempt with the wife retaining $2,000,000 in Trust A. The wife dies in 2007 and her assets are added to the assets in Trust B. There is no estate or generation-skipping transfer tax on either death.

Instead of the trusts terminating and going outright to the couple's two children the assets stay in two equal trusts (a separate trust for each child). The children receive the income from the trust for their lifetimes and at their deaths, the trust continues for their children, the trustors' grandchildren.

This type of trust can run for several generations or longer. Since future generations, the children and their descendents, do not have the right to change the trust or leave assets at their deaths to anyone, the assets are not subject to future estate taxes. Since the assets were exempt at the couple's death from generation-skipping transfer taxes, they will not be subject to these taxes in the future.

How long can such a trust or trusts run? Many states, including California, have laws prohibiting trusts, other than charitable trusts, from continuing forever. Most states have a law referred to as the "rule against perpetuities."[32] Under this law, a trust can continue for the lifetime of everyone alive when the trust became irrevocable, plus an additional 21 years. If John and Mary Doe have children, grandchildren, and possibly great grandchildren living when they each die, the trust can last until the last of their descendents, who were living when they passed away, die, plus an additional 21 years. This can be over 100 years.

Alternatively, many states, including California, provide that a trust can exist for a minimum of 90 years from the time the person died, no matter who survives.[33]

A number of states have abolished this "rule against perpetuities" and a trust can exist forever under the laws of these states. Delaware is one state that

---

[32] California Probate Code section 21200-21231.   [33] California Probate Code sections 21200-21231.

has done this and many major banks have set up trust departments in Delaware to handle these types of trusts.

The advantage of a long-term trust is that the beneficiaries receive earnings and, in some cases, the principal of the trust can also be used for his or her health, support, and maintenance. Divorce, death, bankruptcy, etc. are not a concern, since creditors of a beneficiary or others cannot reach the assets of the trust.

In most cases, a bank or trust company be used because the trustors are unsure as to who will be able to act as trustee over the next 80-100 years.

For couples with larger estates, this type of trust bears consideration.

¶1013 Conclusion

Trusts are both important and complicated. This chapter is a short summation of a very involved subject. Trusts allow great flexibility in handling assets and allow someone to have assets held for another person for various reasons. A trust can save estate taxes, avoid probate, avoid the need for a conservatorship, and do a number of other things.

Once the trust becomes irrevocable at death, these terms cannot be changed. It is very important to carefully consider the terms of the trust and to review them regularly, in case changes to the trust is needed.

Chapter 11

BUSINESS ASSETS

¶1100 Introduction

Business interests or assets require a special consideration in the estate planning process. There are generally three major concerns involved. *First* what is the value of the business interest? Since the Internal Revenue Service counts "goodwill" in valuing a business, a business owner cannot just add up the assets and deduct liabilities.

Second, what happens to the business at death? Do you just sell off the equipment, collect monies owed, and pay creditors? Does someone buy it? If so, who is that someone and what is the price?

Third, who inherits the business? John Doe, who owns a multi-million dollar business, has had his son run it for the last 10-20 years. Although the son knows the business and runs it, he has no ownership interest. The father's will leaves everything to his four children, equally, including the business. The son who is involved in the business does not get any reward for running the business. What happens to the business now?

¶1101 Type of Business

What type of business is being operated?

A *sole propietorship* is a business that is owned by one person, frequently using a fictitious business name. The person is the sole owner and his will or living trust controls the business at death.

A *partnership* is an arrangement where several people have joined together to operate a business.

A *general partnership* is a partnership where several people work together, such as a law firm, group of doctors, engineers, or others. They operate under a partnership agreement that frequently provides what happens to a partner's share at death. In most cases, a managing general partner or partners are appointed to handle the operation of the partnership. The partners divide up their profits or losses each year based on a pre-agreed formula.

A *limited partnership* is a partnership that usually invests in real property or other investments. A general partner or partners, operate and control the partnership. The limited partners are investors and have no liability beyond their original investment. They also have no say in the operation of the limited partnership, although in some cases they can replace the general partner. At death, a limited partner can will away or transfer his interest in the partnership, subject to any restrictions in the partnership agreement. A general partner's interest in a limited partnership is generally more restrictive, and cannot be transferred easily. The partnership agreement may provide who becomes a substituted general partner if the general partner dies, becomes disabled, resigns, or is removed.

A *corporation* is an entity organized under the laws of a state, but can operate in other states. The owners of the corporation own shares of stock. Normally, liability is limited to the assets of the corporation and not to the shareholders. To get money out of the corporation, salaries are taken which are deductible against corporate income. The corporation may pay dividends to its shareholders but the dividends are normally not deductible and represent funds that have been taxed to the corporation and when paid, are again taxed to the shareholders. Small corporations generally try to avoid paying dividends. Shares of stock can normally be transferred at death, although many times there are restrictions on transfer.

To get around the dividend problem some corporations become a *subchapter S corporation*. This type of corporation is limited to 35 shareholders or less. However, the net income the corporation earns each year is not taxed to the corporation but is instead taxed to the shareholders, in relation to their percentage ownership of the corporation.[1] Here, there is no double taxation since income is only taxed individually to the shareholders. A subchapter S corporation has some limitations including problems with irrevocable trusts owning shares. Individuals, estates, and revocable trusts can own shares of stock without problems.

A *limited liability company* is an organization that operates like a general partnership but with limited liability for the shareholders. It is taxed for income tax purposes like a partnership, without all of the restrictions involved. The shareholders enter into a management agreement to appoint a manager for the company. Shares of stock may be transferred at death or the transfer may be restricted, depending upon the agreement of the parties.

¶1102 Valuation

What is the value of the business? This obviously becomes an important concern at someone's death since there will be an estate tax if there is not a surviving spouse, and the valuation will establish a new cost basis for income tax purposes.

An owner of a business may not be the best source to determine value. He or she may view the business as being worth a million dollars if he or she wishes to sell it, but nothing if he or she dies. The Internal Revenue Service may take exception to this valuation.

Usually the accountant is the best one to determine value. The accountant is aware of the valuation problems at death and is also aware of the Internal Revenue Service's position in valuing a business at death.

The Internal Revenue Service looks at several factors in determining the value of a business. These include:

---

[1] Internal Revenue Code section 1366.

1. The nature and history of the business.
2. The economic outlook for the business and industry.
3. The book value and financial condition of the business.
4. The earnings capacity of the business.
5. Any intangible value the business may have.
6. The dividend paying capacity of the business.
7. Prior sales of business ownership by other owners.
8. The market price of similar businesses.

Many times the owners of a business such as a general partnership or corporation will enter into a buy-sell agreement. Under this arrangement, if one owner dies, the remaining owners agree and must buy the deceased owner's interest for a price that is either fixed or based on some formula. If the buy-sell agreement is entered into between parties who are not related, generally the Internal Revenue Service will accept this value.[2]

In some cases, the business is sold after a person's death. If it is sold within one year of the date of death, the Internal Revenue Service will frequently accept the sales price as being the value as of the date of death. If the business is sold after a one year period, it may still be accepted as the sales price, depending upon the circumstances.[3]

In valuing a business, the first place to start is with a "balance sheet." This lists the assets (at cost) and deducts any liabilities. Assets should be increased from their cost (what you paid for the item less depreciation taken for tax purposes) to fair market value (what you could sell the asset for). For trucks, vehicles, and other equipment, this may not result in a significant change. For real estate the difference may be significant. A building may be on the firm's books at $55,000, but currently worth $1,000,000.

To this adjusted figure, *goodwill* is added, which is an intangible based on a going business. The business has a name, history, and reputation. If someone buys it customers likely will continue to come back based on that reputation, even if there is another owner. Goodwill varies significantly depending upon the type of business. Certain retail businesses may continue with a change of ownership but with the same employees and customers may notice little difference. In the case of a doctor or dentist who practices alone, there may be no goodwill left because a new professional will take over the practice.

The other consideration is what happens to the business after death. The federal estate tax return is due nine months from the date of death, but an extension of an additional six months can be obtained. Thus, the return may not be filed for up to 15 months after death. The Internal Revenue Service then has up to three years to audit the return.[4] If the return is audited two years after it is filed, the government then is looking at the business some 39 months after death. If the business has increased in value the Service will then consider a high value

---

[2] Internal Revenue regulation 20.2031-3.
[3] Internal Revenue regulation 20.2031-1(b).

[4] Internal Revenue Code section 6501(a).

---

at date of death. If the business has been closed down, then obviously a low value is in order. While the value is controlled by date of death, this "hindsight" rule allows the tax authorities to look back at the transaction at a later date to determine what happened to the business in the roughly three years after death.

¶1103 Minority Interest

In valuing a business interest or real estate, the federal government has allowed a discount in the value when the decedent held a minority interest, or less than 50% of the total value, or any fractional interest less than 100%.

Over the years, John Doe and his wife transfer 55% of the business to their children. At death, John Doe only owns 45%. Because he has a minority interest a discount is applied. This discount can run from 15-50%, depending upon the nature of the business and other factors. If the business were valued at $10,000,000, no one would pay 45% of that amount or $4,500,000 for less than a 50% ownership because they could not control the business. If a 40% discount was applied, the value would drop to $2,700,000, a discount of $1,800,000, and a potential estate tax savings of up to $850,000.

If John Doe owned 80% of the business, a discount would still apply, but would be a smaller discount than if John Doe owned 49% or less of the business.

¶1104 Business Interest at Death

What happens to the business interest at death?

If the business was a going business as opposed to an investment and there are several owners, then a sale to one or more of the other owners is possible. A buy-sell agreement is a written agreement between owners that provides at the death of an owner the other owners are obligated to buy the deceased person's interest. The formula for the purchase can either be an agreed upon price or a price based on some formula, such as several times the average annual earnings of the business for the last three to five years.

John Doe dies owning 20% of a business, whether a corporation, general partnership or limited liability company. The owners of the remaining 80% agree to buy the deceased person's interest for $100,000. This amount may be paid in cash, or paid partially in cash and partially by a note for the balance, paid over some period of time with interest.

If a corporation or limited liability company is involved, the corporation or company (rather than the other shareholders) may purchase the deceased person's interest. In any case, the results are the same.

To fund this buy-sell agreement, life insurance is frequently purchased by the other owners or by the business entity to pay all or a portion of the purchase price at death.

The buy-sell agreement is the easiest way of handling the valuation and transfer of a business interest at death. The price is fixed and, if the purchasers are not related to the deceased seller, the Internal Revenue Service will normally accept the valuation. The buy out is funded in some way, usually with life insurance, so there either is a cash payout or a large cash down payment, with the balance paid over a period of time.

If there is no buy sell agreement and the business will continue on at death then it may be necessary to obtain the service of a specialized appraisal firm which has the expertise to value this type of business. This would be particularly true of a family business where the decedent owned a majority interest but the business continued on after death, with the children inheriting and running the business. There would be no sale, so valuation will be important.

There could be a possibility that a major competitor or a large, national corporation will buy the business. John Doe owns a chain of 10 successful grocery stores. At his death, no one has the expertise to continue the operation. A sale to a major grocery chain is in order. What should be the sales price? An immediate appraisal is important. Generally, the attorney or accountant would be the one to recommend appraisal services.

Occasionally, a decedent has a key employee or several key employees who may be the best source for purchase of the business. To obtain a value of their services, the business can be valued with the key employees and without the key employess. In this type of situation, financing may be important and the key employees may have little cash to pay down, requiring a payout over some period of time.

If the business continues with a child or other family member running it and it is not sold, where does the money come from to pay estate taxes? Here, life insurance may be purchased and used. Life insurance is not taxable for income tax purposes. It is taxable for estate tax purposes if the decedent was the owner of the policy. However, it is possible for someone else to own the policy or policies, in which case the insurance will normally not be taxable for estate tax purposes.

John Doe has a business worth $10,000,000. Along with other assets, his tax rate is 45% so that $4,500,000 tax would be due in connection with the business. His child or children takes out a life insurance policy for $3,000,000 on the father's life, owning the policy. At death, the insurance proceeds are not taxable for estate or income tax purposes, and the $3,000,000 can be paid to the Internal Revenue Service as a partial payment on the estate tax with the balance paid over a 10 year period.

In a few cases there is no market for the business, and it is liquidated. No one would buy a car repair business where the decedent and one employee did all of the work. The employee lacks the ability and cash to run the business. The assets in terms of equipment and trucks are sold, the accounts receivables collected, and all debts paid. Here, the only value of the business is the net collected after payment of debts.

¶1105 Estate Planning

The first concern is what happens to the business at death. If there is a buy-sell agreement with other owners, then the business interest will be sold at death.

If there is no buy-sell agreement, what happens? The decedent's will or living trust will control the disposition of the business. Does the business go to one child who worked in it and other assets go to other children? Does the business go to all of the children with provision that the child who worked there can buy it for either the value at the date of death or some predetermined value?

No one answer will suffice but the owner needs to review and plan what he or she wants done with the business at death. Is the purchase of life insurance useful to reduce the tax liability?

A sole proprietorship will frequently terminate at death because no one wishes to purchase the business. If the business has a value, such as an accountancy practice, it may be sold. An individual sold one accountancy practice whereby the firm that purchased it agreed to pay 20% of the monies collected from the deceased accountant's clients per year for a five-year period. Approximately 80% of the clients stayed with the new firm, and over the years, the widow received nearly $200,000.

A limited partner usually leaves his or her interest to someone by will or living trust. While it may be difficult to fix the value, normally this is an investment and has no sale value.

A general partner's interest depends upon the general partnership agreement. The partnership agreement may provide a buy-sell arrangement at death. It may also convert the general partner's interest to a limited partner's interest, or, the successor to the general partner may take over. The partnership agreement should be reviewed carefully to see what is provided and, if nothing, it may be necessary to amend the partnership agreement.

A corporation, subchapter S corporation, or limited liability company frequently does not restrict ownership. There may or may not be a buy-sell agreement. If there is none, then the decedent's interest may be controlled by his or her will or living trust. If he or she had a majority interest, the control of the business may pass by the will or trust.

If there is a subchapter S corporation involved, care should be taken if a living trust is used. A subchapter S corporation can have up to 35 shareholders. An irrevocable living trust may not own shares in a subchapter S corporation for more than two years unless the living trust meets the requirements as a qualified subchapter S trust. This means the trust must contain certain provisions. If it does not then the subchapter S election is voided and the corporation becomes a standard corporation. Anyone using a living trust with a subchapter S corporation that will continue with an irrevocable trust after death, needs to have the attorney draft special provisions in the living trust.

A living trust can be used with most business interests. A sole proprietorship, limited partnership interest, shares in a corporation, subchapter S corporation (as long as a revocable trust) and limited liability company all can be transferred to such a trust, if the business entity allows this.

A general partnership interest is different. The partnership agreement may have to be amended to provide for a trust to be a general partner. This may or may not be appropriate depending upon the type and nature of the business.

If a trust owns a business, it is important that the trust agreement or will (for a testamentary trust) authorize the trustee to do this. If the trust is still revocable, then it can be amended to add the necessary provisions. If it is irrevocable and cannot be amended, it may be possible to petition the local Superior Court to allow this.

Prior to death, gifts of a portion of an interest in a business may be utilized. Husband and wife can give $22,000 jointly, each year, to each of their children and grandchildren. If the grandchildren are minors, the gifts can be made under the California Uniform Transfers to Minors Act.[5] Shares of stock or limited partnership interest can be transferred.

The discount provision, which was previously discussed, applies to gifts as well as interests at death. John and Mary Doe transfer stock in a corporation or limited partnership interests. The business is valued. Instead of transferring $22,000 to each child or grandchild, the parties transfer $33,000 worth of stock or interest in the business to each. $33,000 minus a 33% discount equals approximately $22,000. A larger discount may be possible but needs to be examined carefully, usually with the person's accountant.

Over the years this additional 33% allows a much larger amount to be transferred to family members. It may even be appropriate to use part or all of the $1,000,000 lifetime gift tax exemption for each of the spouses for gifts. An 80-year old man owns 80% of a machine manufacturing business. His total estate is slightly over $3,000,000, but his share of the business, which is run by his two sons, is worth $1,000,000 but is rapidly increasing. He gives the business to his son and uses $1,000,000 of his wife's and his own tax exemption. No tax is due. Future appreciation of the business is now out of his estate and belongs to his sons. He has two other children and adjusts his will and living trust to attempt to equalize the value of this gift for his other two children.

¶1106 Community Property

Since most business interests are community property, what happens if the spouse, who is not active in the business, dies first? If a living trust is used, all or part of the business interest goes into Trust B and the surviving spouse can be the trustee and manage it.

In one such case, the wife died first. Half of the community property, which represented half of an auto parts corporation, went into a living trust with a bank as the trustee. The bank as trustee owned one-fourth of the stock, the surviving husband owned one-fourth of the stock, and the other owner owned one-half. Because of conflicts among the people involved, the business was finally dissolved, with a significant loss for everyone.

Any estate plan should take into account the possibility of the non-managing spouse dying first.

---

[5] California Probate Code sections 3900-3925.

¶1107 Family Limited Partnership

A popular estate planning vehicle is to establish a family limited partnership. This is a limited partnership, and the asset or assets of the partnership would consist of a business, real estate, farm, or other investments. The parents would establish a living trust and the trustees of the living trust would be the general partner. Whoever serves as the trustee would be the general partner so there is no vacancy occasioned by someone's death.

The children and grandchildren are the limited partners. If the grandchildren are minors, an irrevocable trust or transfer under the California Uniform Transfers to Minors Act is used and the limited partners place restrictions on the transfer of assets. Transfers cannot be made other than to family members without the permission of the general partner.

The parents, as trustees of the living trust transfer interests in the assets by way of a limited partnership interest to children and grandchildren. They utilize their annual gift tax exemption of $22,000 per child and grandchild and take a discount for the gifts. The discount is based on the minority interest given, and also based on the restrictions for the limited partners. A 20% discount may be taken for the minority interest and another 20% discount may be taken for the lack of marketability of the limited partnership interest after transfer. Thus, approximately $35,000 per person can be transferred each year before the discount, which would reduce each gift to approximately $22,000.

The income that comes into the partnership each year is divided amongst the parties based on their percentage of ownership. The general partner can take an annual salary, which is paid first, before profits are divided.

When the parents later die, their share of the partnership is valued but only their share. The amounts previously transferred to the children and grandchildren are not taxable. If the parent's interest in the partnership at death is less than 50%, a further discount may be applied. Or, at the first party's death, up to $1,500,000 to $3,500,000, depending on the year of death, in partnership interest is put in Trust B. When the survivor dies the survivor and Trust A may own less than 50% interest and a further discount can be used.

Limited partnership interests with family members allow a great deal of planning, depending upon the parties and the nature of the assets. However, this is generally used with a couple that has significantly more than $3,000,000 of assets and has a high net worth asset consisting of a commercial property, business interest, ranch, or farm. A great deal of tax savings can be accomplished using a properly structured vehicle.

Chapter 12

LIFE INSURANCE, ANNUITIES, AND EMPLOYEE BENEFITS

¶1200 Introduction

Like other types of assets, life insurance, annuities, and employee benefits require special consideration in connection with the estate planning process.

Life insurance generally provides a large amount of cash at death. The policies usually are payable to a named beneficiary and avoid probate.

Annuities, particularly single premium tax deferred annuities, are set up to provide a large cash payment at death, to a named beneficiary. Unlike life insurance, these annuities frequently have a large income tax liability.

"Employee benefits" is a generic term referring to the various types of tax deferred benefits available, primarily for retirement purposes. This term includes corporate pension and profit sharing plans, 401(k) plans, self-employed retirement plans, tax sheltered annuities for teachers and other non-profit employees, and individual retirement accounts—both contributory, rollover, and Roth accounts.

¶1201 Community Property Interests in Benefits

Life insurance, annuities, and employee benefits are usually community property. The determination as to whether these types of assets are community property or separate property depends upon the contributions that go into the premiums or plan.

If John Doe takes out a life insurance policy on his life and pays the premiums with community property funds, then the proceeds at death will be community property, and his surviving spouse will be entitled to at least one-half of the benefits.[1] If the premiums were paid out of the decedent's separate property, then the proceeds would be separate property at death. If paid partially from community funds and partially from separate property, then a portion of the proceeds at death will be community property and a portion will be separate property based on the percentage contribution of funds.

If the proceeds are community property, then one-half of the proceeds belong to the surviving spouse. If the surviving spouse does not claim the benefits, then the surviving spouse is making a gift of half of the proceeds to the beneficiary who receives the policy proceeds.

John Doe takes out a $100,000 life insurance policy on his life and names his mother as the beneficiary. Although the premiums are paid out of community

---

[1] California Family Code section 760.

funds, his wife does not demand her half of the policy proceeds at the time of his death and lets the benefits pass to her mother-in-law. Only one-half of the policy or $50,000 is taxable in the decedent's estate for estate tax purposes. Since the wife owns one-half of the policy, she is making a gift of $50,000 to her mother-in-law at the time of her husband's death.

By federal statute, a few policies, primarily federal policies, such as veteran's life insurance or some federal government policies, are the separate property of the insured, and state community property laws do not apply to these policies.

Pension, profit sharing, 401(k), and other plans may also be community property. Here, all or a portion of the contributions are made by the employer. The employer's contribution is treated the same as salary. If the employee is married, the contribution is treated as community property.[2] If the employer pays a portion or all of the life insurance premiums, the premiums are fringe benefits and treated as if the employee received the funds. Again, if the employee is married, the contributions or premiums are community property.

If estate planning is being done for a husband and wife, beneficiary designation must be analyzed very carefully if the spouse or a trust for the spouse is not named as the beneficiary.

Federal law provides that if a couple has been married for one year or longer, and if one spouse is covered by a corporate pension or profit sharing plan, the other spouse *must* be named as beneficiary or that spouse must waive his or her right to the benefits in writing. If one spouse is covered by a pension plan with payments after death, at death the pension must provide that the surviving spouse can elect a joint and survivor's pension unless the spouse waives this in writing.[3]

The federal law only applies to corporate plans and self-employed retirement plans. It does not apply to individual retirement accounts.[4]

¶1202 Beneficiary Designation

All of the plans provide for the naming of a beneficiary upon the death of the insured, annuitant, or participant. John Doe dies and his insurance company is only concerned about who is designated as the beneficiary of his insurance policy. If the primary beneficiary is deceased, then benefits will be paid to the secondary beneficiary or beneficiaries, if any. If there are no living beneficiaries, then the benefits will be paid to the insured's or participant's estate.

Most people tend to ignore or forget whom they name as beneficiary. Frequently, people will think it is their spouse and then their children. After death, it is discovered that the decedent "guessed," and the benefits are payable to someone else. Sometimes one child is named instead of all of the children because that one child is younger than the others and the parents wanted her to receive a larger share at death. Thirty years later, when the parent dies her age is

---

[2] California Family Code section 2610.   [4] Internal Revenue Code section 401(a)(11)(B).
[3] Internal Revenue Code section 401(a)(11).

no longer relevant but the beneficiary is unchanged and the one daughter receives an additional $50,000 more than the other children.

People should carefully examine life insurance, annuities and employee benefits and get a written statement about who is the designated beneficiary. If there is any question about the beneficiary or beneficiaries, a new beneficiary form should be obtained, completed, and given to the company or trustee. A copy of the beneficiary designation should be retained.

¶1203 Life Insurance

Life insurance is important in estate planning. It usually represents a large cash benefit that is available within 30-60 days after death. It avoids probate because it is payable to a named beneficiary. If a couple uses a living trust, the trust is usually named as the beneficiary since the insurance policy becomes cash at death.

.01 Parties to a Life Insurance Contract

There are several parties to a life insurance policy.

The *owner* of the policy is the person who controls the policy. The owner names the beneficiary, can borrow against the policy, elect any benefits, and take all legal action in connection with the policy. In most cases the insured is also the owner. Completing an assignment form and submitting it to the insurance company may change ownership of life insurance. A few policies, such as veteran's insurance, cannot be assigned and must remain in the insured's name.

If the owner is different from the insured, and if the owner dies before the insured, who inherits the ownership of the policy? A form can be filled out and filed with the insurance company designating a new owner. If this is not done, then the deceased owner's will controls who inherits the policy.

The *insured* is the person whose life is covered by the policy. Insurance may be owned by someone other than the insured. Upon the death of the insured, the insurance company will pay the benefits stipulated in the insurance contract or policy. The insured does not change during the life of the policy.

The *beneficiary* is the person or entity who receives the policy proceeds upon the death of the insured. If the beneficiary is not living, the proceeds do not go to the beneficiary's estate but go to the next named beneficiary. If no named beneficiary is alive at the insured's death, the policy proceeds are paid to the policy owner's estate. The beneficiary is selected by the policy owner, not the insured, and can be changed at any time, unless the beneficiary designation is irrevocable, which is extremely rare.

.02 Taxability of Life Insurance

Are life insurance proceeds taxable for income or estate tax purposes? No and yes.

Life insurance proceeds are normally not taxable for income tax purposes. The Internal Revenue Code specifically exempts life insurance proceeds from income tax.[5]

The only exemption is if the policy is sold for value. John Doe "sells" his life insurance policy to his son for $5,000. The policy then becomes an investment and is taxable at death for income tax purposes over the amount paid for the policy including premium payments.

With regard to estate tax, life insurance is normally taxable.[6] Mary Doe has a $50,000 life insurance policy on her life payable to her three children. At her death, the three children collect the life insurance without probate and without income tax. However, the $50,000 is added to all of the decedent's other assets for estate tax purposes. If the total is over $1,500,000 to $3,500,000 depending on the year of death, it is taxable.

If the owner of a life insurance policy is not the insured, then the proceeds are not taxable.[7] The $50,000 policy on the life of Mary Doe is owned by her three children, and not by Mary Doe. The policy proceeds will generally not be taxable. The exception to this rule is if the insured transferred the policy within three years of death.[8] If the policy is transferred by the insured and he or she dies within three years, the policy proceeds are still taxed in the insured's estate at death. If the transfer occurs more than three years before death, the policy proceeds are not taxable.

The only time a gift tax issue arises is if the owner transfers a life insurance policy to someone prior to the insured's death. The value of the gift is the terminable reserve value of the policy. If the policy has no significant cash value, this is generally rather low. The gift of a life insurance policy is a present interest gift and qualifies for the $11,000 per year gift tax exemption.

.03 Estate Planning with Life Insurance

How is life insurance handled? If a couple has less than $3,000,000, including life insurance, a living trust will cover the estate tax problems, and no special procedures are generally required. If a single person has less than $1,500,000 including life insurance, there are no problems.

What if the couple or individual has a larger amount and has life insurance? An assignment of the life insurance to a new owner may be appropriate. If there is an existing policy and that policy is assigned, it must be transferred at least three years before death to avoid estate tax.

Who should be the owners? Generally the people who receive the proceeds at death should be the owners. John Doe is a widower with an estate of over $2,000,000, including $100,000 of life insurance. If he removes the $100,000 policy from his taxable estate at death, there will be an estate tax savings of approximately $45,000. He can assign or transfer the policy to his children. If he dies within three years, the tax is no greater than if he had not made the assignment.

---

[5] Internal Revenue Code section 101(a).
[6] Internal Revenue Code section 2042.

[7] Internal Revenue Code section 2042(2).
[8] Internal Revenue Code section 2035.

The only concern, on the transfer or assignment of an insurance policy to individuals, is regarding what happens if the owner or owners die before the insured. John Doe transfers his $100,000 policy to his three children, who are also the beneficiaries of the policy. One of his sons dies before the father. The son's one-third interest in the policy passes by the son's will to the son's wife. At the father's later death, the daughter-in-law collects one-third of the insurance proceeds. She later remarries, and the insurance may not ultimately go to the insured's grandchildren.

If the children own the father's life insurance, it may be subject to their creditors or possible bankruptcy in the event the children have financial problems.

One alternative is to establish an irrevocable trust to own the policy and collect the proceeds. Although the insurance may be used to pay the estate tax, the trust cannot legally require the trustee to pay this tax obligation.[9] If it does, the proceeds will be taxable for estate tax purposes because the trust is paying a legal obligation of the decedent at death.

The disadvantage of an irrevocable life insurance trust is the complexity. There needs to be a trustee, and the person setting up the trust cannot be the trustee. Records must be kept and an annual income tax return must be filed. When the insured dies and the policy proceeds are collected, they must be invested and work must be done on the payment of the insured's estate tax.

The trust would not normally qualify for the $11,000 per year per donee gift tax exemption. To qualify, Crummey provisions (discussed in Chapter 8) are put in the trust document. The value of the gift is the value of the policy. Future premium payments are usually made by the insured by way of a gift to the trust.

John Doe establishes an irrevocable trust with a son as trustee and his four children as the beneficiaries. He transfers a $500,000 life insurance policy that has a value of less than $40,000. He can contribute $44,000 per year ($11,000 per child) for payment of premium. If his wife is alive, she can also contribute $44,000 per year.

The trustee receives the gifts and makes the premium payments. If the father lives three or more years after transfer of the life insurance, at his death the policy proceeds are not taxable for estate tax purposes.

A variation is to have an irrevocable trust take out a new life insurance on the insured's life. If the trust takes out a new policy as the original owner, then no three-year period is involved and if the insured dies within three years, the policy proceeds are not taxable. Here, a new life insurance policy may be purchased if the insured is in good health, can get a policy, and the premiums are economically feasible.

If a child dies before the parent/insured, the trust determines what happens to the child's share. If the trustee dies, a successor trustee is named. The trust may even be a generation skipping trust, continuing for the grandchildren after the children's deaths. The trust allows a great deal of flexibility. It is irrevocable

---

[9] Internal Revenue Code section 2042(2).

so all decisions must be made before the trust is established. Changes cannot be made after the trust has been established.

.04 Joint and Survivor Life Insurance

With husband and wife there are generally no estate taxes due until the death of the second spouse. A popular life insurance product in recent years is a *joint and survivor* life insurance policy.

This is a policy that insures both husband and wife but pays upon the death of the surviving spouse. The premiums are lower although they continue for a longer period of time. Because of the lower premiums, the full gift tax exemption can be used if the policy is given away prior to death. The second advantage is that both spouses are being insured. Health problems for one spouse will generally not create problems if the other spouse qualifies. It is much easier to qualify a couple for life insurance than a single person.

A couple has a taxable estate of $5,000,000. Even with a living trust, a tax of more than $900,000 will be due on the death of the second spouse. An irrevocable trust is established which purchases life insurance on the couple's joint lives. Upon the death of the second spouse $1,000,000 is payable to the trust. The estate tax is then paid from tax-free money since there is no income or estate tax on the life insurance proceeds.

While life insurance is not for everyone, it should be a consideration in large estates, particularly with those that lack liquidity. If combined with an irrevocable trust, it can significantly decrease the estate tax costs.

¶1204 Annuities

An annuity is a contract whereby an individual gives a sum of money to an annuity company and the company pays a monthly amount to the individual for life. There are numerous variations that pay for a minimum of 5, 10, or 20 years, or for some guaranteed period of time. If the individual dies before this period, the annuity continues to the named beneficiary until the end of the period.

An immediate annuity starts upon the receipt of the money and the issuance of the contract.

One variation of the annuity that has become very popular in recent years is a *single premium tax-deferred annuity*. Here, a sum of money is given to the annuity company. The company invests the money, and the earnings and appreciation accumulate without tax. If money is drawn, income tax on the money withdrawn must be paid until tax on all of the earnings and accumulation have been paid. At some point in the individual's life, one must convert the deferred annuity into a present annuity and start withdrawing the funds, usually by age 80, 85, or 90. The advantage is that everything accumulates tax free.

.01 Parties to an Annuity Contract

There are various parties involved with an annuity contract, similar to a life insurance policy.

The *annuitant* is the person whose life is covered. He or she may or may not be the owner. Mary Doe is 86 and wants to establish a single premium tax-deferred annuity. Because she is too old for an annuity, she takes out the annuity on the life of her granddaughter, who is 26 years of age. Mary, however, is the owner of the policy.

The death of the annuitant triggers the payment of the balance of the annuity, subject to certain options in the annuity contract.

The *owner* is the person who owns and controls the annuity. Much like life insurance, the owner can name a beneficiary, withdraw funds, cancel the policy, or take any other legal action. If the owner dies before the annuitant, a new owner is usually designated. If a new owner is not designated then the deceased owner's will covers who inherits the policy.

The *beneficiary* is the person or entity who receives the annuity upon the death of the annuitant. The beneficiary is named by the owner of the annuity contract. There can be several beneficiaries who divide up the proceeds, or a primary and secondary beneficiary. If no beneficiary survives, the proceeds pass to the owner or owner's estate.

.02 Taxation of Annuity

The taxation of an annuity is different from the taxation of a life insurance policy.

Income Tax. If a person purchases a regular annuity with monthly or periodic payments, then a portion of each payment is a return of investment and is tax free, and the portion that is earnings, is taxable. The numbers are determined by the Internal Revenue Code and regulations, which set out a formula for determining this.[10]

A single premium deferred annuity is taxable when the funds from the annuity are received. Everything over and above the original investment is taxable.[11] John Doe purchases a single premium deferred annuity for $10,000. Many years later he cashes it in and receives $25,000. The difference, $15,000, is taxable as ordinary income. If a deferred variable annuity contract was purchased prior to October 21, 1979, then the proceeds at death are not subject to any income tax.[12]

Older tax-deferred annuities allowed borrowing against the policy. The former tax law allowed principal to be borrowed out first. In the prior example John Doe could have borrowed $10,000 from the policy and not paid any income tax. Unfortunately, the tax law was changed and any annuities purchased after August 12, 1982 do not allow this.[13] Older policies did and still do permit such tax-free borrowing. Now, any borrowing triggers taxable income up to the total taxable income in the policy.[14]

Most assets get a new value at death and any appreciation is forgiven. This general rule does not extend to annuity policies.[15] John Doe has invested $10,000 in a deferred annuity that is worth $25,000 at his death. He names his two

---

[10] Internal Revenue Code section 72.
[11] Internal Revenue Code section 72(b).
[12] Revenue Ruling 79-335.

[13] Internal Revenue Code section 72(p).
[14] Internal Revenue Code section 72(p)(1)(A).
[15] Internal Revenue Code section 1014(b)(9)(A).

children as the beneficiaries, which avoids probate. The children cash in the policy and receive $25,000. They still must pay income tax on the $15,000 appreciation since the policy was purchased. The earnings on an annuity policy may be deferred for a period of time but they will always be taxable at some point to someone.

Estate Tax. The death of the owner causes the value of the policy to be taxed in the owner's estate for federal estate tax purposes.[16]

John Doe dies and has a single premium tax-deferred annuity policy. Although he originally invested $50,000, the policy is worth $125,000 at the time of death. For estate tax purposes, the $125,000 is added to the decedent's other assets

If the annuitant dies and the annuitant and the owner are separate parties, the death of the annuitant does not trigger any federal estate tax. Mary Doe takes out a $50,000 annuity in which she is the owner but her daughter is the annuitant. The daughter dies and the policy is worth $75,000. Because the daughter does not own the policy, it is not subject to estate tax.

Gift Tax. A gift tax liability arises if an owner of an annuity transfers the policy ownership to another person. Here, the value of the gift is the value of the policy at the time of the transfer. If the value is over $11,000, a gift tax return is due.

Unfortunately, the income tax liability cannot be given away. If there is taxable income in the policy, then at the time of transfer, the donor/owner must *also* pay income tax on the taxable income in the policy.[17]

Mary Doe invests $25,000 in a policy. A few years later the policy is worth $35,000. She completes an assignment form and transfers the policy to her daughter as the new owner. She has made a gift of $35,000 to her daughter. She (not the daughter) is liable for income tax on the $10,000 increase in value at the time of gift. When the policy is later cashed in, the income tax cost basis is $35,000, and income tax is then paid on the excess received by the daughter.

¶1205 Employee Benefits

The term "employee benefits" is used to include all of the various plans that allow the deferral of income for an employee. These include a corporate pension, profit sharing, or 401(k) plan, tax sheltered annuities and other deferred benefits of teachers and other government employees, tax deferred benefits of employees of non-profit organizations, individual retirement accounts (contributory, rollover and Roth) and self-employed retirement plans (referred to as Keogh or HR-10 plans).

Virtually all of these plans allow monies to be set aside on a tax deferred basis, allow the funds to accumulate tax free, and the monies or assets are then made subject to income tax when they are distributed to the employee, presumably after retirement.

---

[16] Internal Revenue Code section 2039.   [17] Internal Revenue Code section 72(p)(1)(B).

Although the plans may be community property in nature, the non-participant spouse has no control over the plan. John Doe has a $150,000 profit sharing plan through his corporation. At his death he can name a beneficiary to receive the benefits. However, if his wife dies before he does, she cannot pass any of the benefits at death. Although the benefits may be community property, under federal law she cannot have any right to dispose of the benefits if she dies before her husband. The non-participant cannot control any benefits. The plan can only provide for payment to the employee, participant or to a named beneficiary at death.

.01 Parties to Plan Benefits

The *participant* or *employee* is the person covered by the plan. He or she is treated as the owner and is the person covered.

The *beneficiary* is the person or people named to receive the benefits upon the death of the participant/employee. In a corporate plan, the spouse, if married for more than one year, must be named as the beneficiary unless the spouse waives this right in writing. If the contributions made to the plan were made for a married person during marriage, they will be considered incidental to employment, and the plan benefits based on these contributions will be community or quasi-community property. In either case, the spouse is entitled to one-half of the benefits at death, even if the spouse has not been the named beneficiary.

.02 Income Tax

Since virtually all of the contributions made to these plans are tax deductible, either by the individual or the corporation, they are taxable when received from the plan.

There are various laws and regulations about when the plan benefits must be withdrawn. For an individual retirement account, the participant must start drawing benefits based on one of several formulas by April 1 of the year following the year in which the participant attained age 70-1/2.[18] If the participant dies and the benefits are paid to the named beneficiary, either in a lump sum or over a period of time, the benefits are taxable as withdrawn as ordinary income.

There are special rules if the decedent's spouse was the named beneficiary. The spouse, but only the spouse, may rollover the plan benefits to a new IRA account in the spouse's name without any income tax liability.[19] The new rollover IRA account then belongs to the spouse who must withdraw funds based on the spouse's age. If the spouse does not rollover the benefits, the spouse must withdraw the funds over a specific period of time and pay income tax on the funds as withdrawn.[20]

If the participant dies, the benefits can normally be paid over a period of time if the beneficiary is a person or persons and not trust. If a trust is the named

---

[18] Internal Revenue Code section 401(a)(9)(C).
[19] Internal Revenue Code section 401(a)(9)(B)(iv).
[20] Internal Revenue Code section 401(a)(9).

beneficiary, then the benefits normally must be paid out over a period of not more than five years.[21]

Even though the benefits are taxable for income tax purposes, they also may be taxable for estate tax purposes. To avoid double taxation, the Internal Revenue Code allows an income tax deduction for the estate tax attributable to the benefits that are also taxable for income tax purposes. This is not a tax credit but merely an itemized deduction for what is referred to as *income with respect to a decedent*.[22] This deduction usually works out to be a relatively small amount.

These types of plans merely defer the tax. The benefits must be withdrawn in time and when withdrawn, are taxable for income tax purposes.

.03 Estate Tax

If the participant or employee dies, the benefits which are payable at death are fully taxable for estate tax purposes. The value is the current fair market value of the plan or the plan's assets as of the date of death.[23] If the benefits are payable to the surviving spouse who is a United States citizen, they are exempt from estate tax.[24]

If the decedent, a widower, left $1,500,000 in a rollover IRA account payable to his children, the benefits would be added to the decedent's other assets. The tax could be over 45%, or $675,000 on this IRA. If money is drawn out of the IRA to pay the tax, the money is also then taxable for income tax purposes.

.04 Gift Tax

Because of the nature of these plans, the participant rarely makes a gift. John Doe has $500,000 in a plan. He cannot transfer the benefits to someone. He can withdraw the benefits, in which case he is liable for the income tax on the funds distributed to him. He can then give away the balance. However, he cannot escape the income tax by transferring the plan to someone.

¶1206 Estate Planning

Estate planning for the previously mentioned benefits is rather complex. For life insurance, a living trust may be named as the beneficiary since there is no income tax. If the couple or individual's estate is large, a transfer of life insurance, or the purchase of new life insurance with children or an irrevocable trust or others as the owner and beneficiary, may be desirable to eliminate or reduce the potential estate tax.

Annuities are more complex because of the income tax liability. If a trust is named as the beneficiary, the trust must collect the monies within a certain period of time and pay the tax. Trust income tax rates are high. An individual may be named as the beneficiary and that individual may spread out payments and reduce the income tax.

Employee benefits are normally payable to the spouse, if there is one, and then payable directly to children or others. No estate tax is payable upon the

---

[21] Internal Revenue Code section 401(a)(9)(B)(ii).   [23] Internal Revenue Code section 2031.

[22] Internal Revenue Code section 61(a)(14).   [24] Internal Revenue Code section 2056.

participant's death if the spouse in named primary beneficiary. The spouse can rollover the plan distributions to a new rollover IRA account and initially avoid income tax. If children receive the benefits, there may be estate tax, but the children can take out the benefits over a period of time, minimizing the potential income tax.

All of this is well and good if the couple has $3,000,000 of other assets and can fully fund the $1,500,000 estate tax exemption at death. But what happens if a couple has $2,000,000 of community property and the husband has a $1,000,000 rollover IRA account. While the $2,000,000 of community property can be placed in a living trust, if either spouse dies only one-half or $1,000,000 can be sheltered. $500,000 of the estate tax exemption is lost. If the IRA account is payable to the trust no estate tax is due but it does trigger a massive income tax and some excise tax. If the wife dies first, none of the IRA can go into the living trust. In this situation the couple will probably elect to have the IRA paid to the spouse and then to the children as beneficiaries. As funds are withdrawn during their lifetimes and income tax is paid, these funds can then be added to the living trust. While benefits may be paid to an irrevocable trust and withdrawn over a period of time, the rules are very complex.[25]

An alternative is to have a written agreement allowing a non-prorata division of the total community property. With a written agreement the $1,000,000 IRA account can be counted in dividing the trust assets, allowing either spouse at the first death to shelter $1,500,000 (one-half of $2,000,000 community property trust assets and $1,000,000 IRA account).

There is no single right way to designate a beneficiary for these benefits. A beneficiary should be designated after discussing all of the tax implications with a professional and determining the various options and tax under each option. The individual or couple can then make a decision as to who will be named as beneficiary or beneficiaries.

---

[25] Internal Revenue regulations 1.401(a)(9)-2.

Chapter 13

MISCELLANEOUS ASSETS

¶1300 Introduction

Certain assets require careful consideration to avoid tax or probate problems. These types of assets can include real property in another state or country, furniture and personal effects, collections of various types, installment obligations, United States savings bonds, and others.

¶1301 Assets in Another State or Country

Real property must be administered at death in accordance with the laws of the state or country where the real estate is located. Oregon will not allow California to make laws regarding the disposition of Oregon real estate.

If the decedent owned real estate in Oregon but was a California resident at the time of death, a probate may be necessary in California and an ancillary or another probate may also be necessary in Oregon with regard to the Oregon real property.

If a living trust is used, even if in another state, normally the real estate can be transferred into the living trust to avoid probate at death.

The rights, with regard to real property, are determined by the laws where the real estate is located. Oregon is not a community property state, so any real estate owned by husband and wife in Oregon cannot be community property. Each spouse may own one-half of the real property as his or her separate property. Only one-half of the real estate gets a new cost basis at death rather than both halves, as under California community property law.[1]

Personal property, which is all assets except real estate, is handled by the state of domicile of the decedent.[2] If John Doe died and was a California resident, his bank account in Oregon would be handled by the probate in California but real estate in Oregon would be handled in Oregon.

To avoid probate, an individual or couple can use a living trust or place property in joint tenancy.

Assets in another country also present problems. Each country is protective of its assets, and the term "assets" includes real estate, securities, or a business organized in that country. If a person owns real estate in France and dies as a resident of California, a probate may also be necessary in France to pass title with regard to the French real estate. French law will govern as to the French real estate.

---

[1] Internal Revenue Code section 1014(a)(1).　　　[2] California Probate Code section 9650.

If the decedent was a citizen of the United States or permanent United States resident, he or she is taxed for federal estate tax purposes on all of his or her assets anywhere in the world.[3] The French real estate would be taxed by the United States and would also be subject to French death tax. However, the United States would allow a credit for all or a portion of the French tax paid.[4]

Securities in companies organized in another country are also subject to tax. If the decedent owned stock in an English company at the time of death, the English stock would be subject to estate or inheritance tax in England, and also taxed under Unites States estate tax law.

People who own real estate in another state or who own real estate or securities in another country should very carefully plan their estates to avoid probate and to minimize the combined taxes that may be paid at death.

¶1302 Mineral Interests

Many people own mineral interests, particularly ones in another state. These mineral interests, such as oil and gas interests, are considered real property.[5]

If the mineral interests are in another state, then a probate may be required at death if the mineral interests are in the decedent's name alone. Some oil companies will transfer mineral interests after death without probate but will only transfer these interests to the decedent's heirs-at-law, even if there was a will, rather than the beneficiaries under the will, unless the will is probated in that state.

Many people want to change title to their mineral interests. Placing the mineral interests in a living trust, placing the interests in joint tenancy, or making a gift by transferring the mineral interest to someone such as children can only do this.

Unfortunately, the transfer of mineral interests is complicated. Writing the oil company with a request for transfer will normally not be sufficient. It is necessary to record a deed that transfers these interests in the county the mineral interests are located. This process is similar to the transfer of real property. After the deed is recorded, a copy of the deed is provided to the oil company and usually requires some form of an assignment, called a "division order." The client signs the division order, and the title to the mineral rights and the lease by the oil company are then transferred.

Many people do not have the necessary legal description of the mineral interests in order to draft a deed. Sometimes the oil company has a copy, but many times they do not. It is necessary to use a form of deed for the specific state involved (the form of deed varies from state to state), have it recorded in the county where the mineral interests are located, and pay a recording fee. This can become very complicated, even for a California attorney. It is simpler to use a local attorney in the state involved. Many people do not do this because of the complexity and costs involved.

---

[3] Internal Revenue Code section 2001(a).
[4] Internal Revenue Code section 2014.

[5] California Civil Code sections 883.110-883.140.

¶1303 Installment Obligations

An installment obligation is where someone has sold an asset, such as real estate, carried back a note for a portion of the sales price, and elected to pay the capital gains over the period of time rather than pay the tax on all of the gain in the year of sale.

John Doe sells real estate for $400,000. His income tax basis is $40,000, so there will be $360,000 capital gains. Rather than receive the entire $400,000, he elects to receive $40,000 down and have nine annual payments of $40,000 plus interest. Thus, he will receive the $400,000 purchase price over a ten year period rather than all in one year.

Instead of paying the tax on the $360,000 capital gain in the year of sale, he elects to pay a portion each year as he receives a payment. The $360,000 capital gain is 90% of the sales price. Each principal payment he receives will require him to report 90% of the principal payment. The $40,000 down payment will generate a $36,000 capital gain, as will each annual payment. The $360,000 capital gain will still be reported, but spread over a 10 year period rather than reported all in one year.

John Doe dies after four years with $240,000 left as the balance on the loan. This balance of $240,000 is added to other assets which he owns and is subject to federal estate tax. No income tax deduction is allowed for the income tax to be paid on the balance because the payments have not been made and the tax liability only arises as the payments are received. However, this loan or note does not get a new stepped-up income tax cost basis at death.[6]

The person or people who inherit the $240,000 will still have to pay capital gains on the $40,000 annual payments as they are received, just as the decedent did. Thus, the assets are taxed twice, for estate tax and for income tax. An income tax deduction is allowed for the estate tax attributable to the $216,000 gain (90% of $240,000), but this income tax deduction (not a tax credit) is usually rather small.

No real planning can be done once someone enters into an installment obligation. If the installment obligation is given away, the donor not only has to report the balance due on the note for gift tax purposes, but also has to pay the income tax on the future unpaid capital gains.[7] If John Doe gave away the note with a balance of $240,000 before death, he would be making a gift of $240,000 and would also be required to report $216,000 (90% of $240,000) of capital gains on that year's income tax return. The donee would not have any income tax liability in the future for the capital gains.

An installment obligation can be placed in a living trust to avoid probate, but it does not solve the income tax problem. The only way to avoid the tax is to not enter into this sale. If John Doe kept the property until he died and it was valued at $400,000 when he died, then it would get a new income tax basis at death and if sold for $400,000, either outright or via an installment obligation, no capital gains would occur and no tax would be due.

---

[6] Internal Revenue Code section 453B(b).   [7] Internal Revenue Code section 453B(a).

¶1304 United States Savings Bonds

United States savings bonds have been an investment for many years. Originally they were used to help finance World War II. They were issued for 75% of the face value, increasing to the face value after 10 years. The government did not wish to pay them off so they were extended to a maximum of 40 years. Now, 40 years after the date of issue, they quit bearing interest.

"E" bonds accumulate interest and the interest is not received until the bond is cashed. The taxpayer can report the increase in interest each year or, can report the interest when the bond is cashed.[8]

"H" bonds are issued in a fixed amount such as $500 or $1,000. The value of the bond remains fixed and interest, which is taxable, is paid to the bond owner every six months. It is possible to convert the E bonds into H bonds without paying income tax on the accumulation. A notation is then put on the H bonds so that when they are later cashed in the recipient pays income tax on this accumulated interest.

John Doe buys $10,000 of E bonds. The bonds increase in value until they are worth $40,000. John Doe converts the E bonds to H bonds and pays no income tax. He then receives income every six months on the $40,000 of H bonds, which is taxable. If he cashes in any of the H bonds, he will have to pay income tax on this accumulated interest.

The federal government has issued "EE" bonds and "HH" bonds during the last 20 years. These have different maturity dates but the same tax rules apply. There are also other types of United States savings bonds.

The various United States savings bonds may be held in two individual's name as "co-owners." This is nothing more than joint tenancy. If bonds are in the name of John Doe or Mary Doe, and one party dies, the other party can cash in the bonds or have the bonds reregistered. Bonds can also be payable on death, such as in the name of John Doe P.O.D. Mary Doe. At John Doe's death Mary Doe can reregister or cash in the bonds.

The interest on the bonds is taxable for federal income tax purposes but it is exempt from California income tax.[9]

The problem with the bonds, from an estate tax point of view, is that they are subject to estate tax and income tax. John Doe dies owning $40,000 of E bonds in his name alone. The bonds are probated in his estate. The executor cashes in the bonds later discovers that the bonds cost $10,000, so that of the $40,000 received $30,000 is taxable interest. The bonds do not get a new value at death for income tax purposes.

There is little estate planning that can be done. Again, if the bonds are given away, the donor is liable for the income tax on the interest accumulated in the bond at the time of gift. The income tax liability cannot be given to someone.

---

[8] Internal Revenue Code section 454(a).

[9] California Revenue & Taxation Code section 17143.

To avoid probate, the bonds may be placed in a living trust, put in co-ownership with someone, or payable on death to someone. Unfortunately, only two people can be co-owners and only one person can be a beneficiary under a P.O.D. registration. If Mary Doe does not have a living trust and wants the bonds to go to her three children at death, she will have to divide the bonds up into three groups and put one child on each group of bonds.

The only income tax savings that is possible is, in the year of death, to include all of the taxable income, up to the date of death, on the decedent's final income tax return.[10] If there is little other taxable income in the year of death, the tax savings may be significant. When the bonds are cashed, the recipient only pays income tax on the interest from the date of death until the date of redemption.

It is also possible to convert E to H bonds or EE to HH bonds. Although there are no tax savings, future interest is paid out and taxable. The interest up until the conversion date is then frozen and only taxed if the H or HH bonds are cashed.

Lastly, the interest is not taxable until the bonds are cashed. The recipient of the bonds may reregister them and also convert them to H or HH bonds, not paying the income tax until the bonds are cashed at some point in the future.

¶1305 Collectibles

Does the decedent or person doing estate planning have a valuable collection? Many people have collections but it is discovered after death that the value is small.

The controlling factor is the "value" of any collection. The value of a collection is what a willing buyer would pay for the collection.[11] Costs of selling a collection, such as storage and auction fees, generally are not deductible for estate tax purposes.

If a federal estate tax return is filed, the return asks on schedule F of the return "Did the decedent at the time of death own any articles of artistic or collectible value in excess of $3,000 or any collections whose artistic or collectible value combined at date of death exceed $10,000? If 'yes,' submit full details on this schedule and attach appraisals." Stamps, coins, or other types of collections need to be valued to determine if they are likely to have a significant value at death.

A woman was concerned because her deceased husband was a retired professor of art at a major university. He left his wife with about 1,000 paintings, sculptures and other art objects. A careful review determined that none of the items had significant value, and an average value of $40-60 per item would be appropriate.

A widow had a painting given to her 35 years earlier when she and her husband lived in an artists'colony in California. Although the artist was deceased and the widow heard that his paintings were selling, she paid little attention.

[10] Internal Revenue Code section 454(a).   [11] Internal Revenue regulation 20.2031-1.

One of her sons urged her to get the painting valued and she contacted an art gallery. She was stunned to discover that they estimated its sales price at $85,000.

If there is any question as to valuation, an appraiser in that field should be consulted to review and estimate the value. If this value is relatively low, then no written appraisal is needed. An individual has a stamp collection but it is estimated at being worth $500-750 at death. No written appraisal is needed. If it is worth $3,000 or more, a written appraisal should be obtained.

If the decedent had a collection, a professional group, such as the local stamp or coin club, can be contacted to get the name of an appraiser. There are several major auction houses in San Francisco and Los Angeles which have specialists available in virtually any field. They can be contacted particularly if they will be used to sell the item or items at auction.

A man died with a total net estate of approximately $250,000, including the equity in his home. In his garage were approximately 20 bottles of wine. One of the two heirs knew a little about wine and consulted an expert. Later, the wine was sold at auction and netted the estate $5,000 after payment of commissions and costs.

For every story where a valuable article or collection is found, there are 40 or 50 stories about items or collections that people think have value, but which turn out to be worth a great deal less than expected. While an uncle may have thought his stamp collection was worth $50,000, it's discovered after death that it is really only worth $2,500.

The potential sales price is the key element for determining the value of any collection or collections.

¶1306 Furniture, Furnishings, and Vehicles

Furniture, furnishings, vehicles, and personal items need to be handled in accordance with the person's wishes. Many people have no concern with regard to these assets but are happy leaving everything to their children, letting the children decide on how to divide these assets. Some people are more concerned and wish a number of specific items to go to various people.

Most attorneys try to avoid listing a lengthy breakdown on the division of personal assets in a person's will or codicil. If the person's wishes change over the years, or if items are given away before death, then the will has to be changed by codicil. The expense and hassle of drafting a number of codicils for these items can be disproportionate to the value of the items.

Some people put a tag or note on personal items. While this may be practical, it is not legal. There is always the problem of a relative removing or changing the tags. A father, who had four children, put numbered tags on items, with each number representing one of the children. He then locked up the key to the numbers so that no one would know who inherited the items until after his death.

The simplest and most appropriate way to handle personal items is to execute a handwritten codicil to the will. California recognizes a handwritten will or codicil as long as it is in the individual's handwriting, dated, and signed.

No witnesses are required.[12] If the codicil is clear in terms of identifying the items and who receives them, then there are no problems. Any items not listed in the codicil would then be divided up among the parties inheriting the residue of the estate.

The disadvantage of doing this is that if there is a probate and estate tax return, each item must be valued separately. If items are not listed separately in the will or codicil, then a lump sum value is put on the furniture, furnishings, jewelry, and personal effects. If 10 or 15 items are listed, each of those items must be valued and a value placed on the remainder of the furniture, furnishings and personal items. The total value may be greater than if a single value had been ascribed to all of the furniture and furnishings.

Some people go overboard listing items. Only items important to the individual should be listed. Some people itemize pots, pans, bedding and clothing. Others leave 15-page handwritten list of approximately 300 items or more. In terms of jewelry, furniture, heirlooms, or other items, list the important items and clearly identify the item so there are no problems. If a ring is left to someone and 20 rings were owned, it may not be possible to identify the specific ring unless it is described in detail. Be careful of leaving an item "in the bedroom." Upon death, it may not still be in the bedroom, but located elsewhere, and can create problems.

If furniture, jewelry, or other items are wished packed and shipped to someone, one must specify that the estate will pay these costs. If not, the beneficiary must pay these costs. Also, if there is an estate tax, the normal rule is that each beneficiary must pay his or her proportionate share of the tax unless stated otherwise.[13] If a son receives $400,000 of assets and some personal items, the tax on his portion will be deducted from his share. However, if his sister receives jewelry and furniture worth $5,000 and no other assets, she may have to pay $1,000 or more as her share of the estate tax. A way around this is to provide that these bequests are "free" of estate tax. This means that the estate tax would be paid by the other estate beneficiaries.[14] If the items the people are inheriting is fairly low in value, this becomes the easiest solution.

Vehicles, motor homes, mobile homes, motorcycles, and other types of vehicles can be valued by using a "blue book" or other commercial guide that gives a value for the items.

¶1307 Animals

What happens to one's animals at death? Animals are considered property so they can be left to someone. It cannot be directed that an animal be put to death when one dies. Jane Doe wanted her will to state that her German shepherd be put to death and buried in the coffin with her. This is specifically against California law.

It is not legally possible to leave assets to an animal.[15] It is possible to set up a trust to financially care for an animal and then have the trust assets distributed

[12] California Probate Code section 6111.
[13] California Probate Code sections 20110-20117.
[14] California Probate Code section 20110(b)(1).
[15] California Probate Code section 15212.

to relatives, friends, or a charity when the animal dies. It is also possible to leave animals to someone with a cash bequest or other assets for the friend or relative to take care of the animal.

John Doe had three dogs and left them in his will to a friend along with his $300,000 home so that the dogs would have a place to run and play after he died. After the dogs died, the friend got to keep the home. While such an arrangement is somewhat unusual, it is legal.

If there are specific desires, one may wish to leave their dogs, cats, horses, or other animals to a friend or relative with a cash bequest to allow the person to take care of the animal and to pay vet bills and costs. Before doing so it is well to discuss this with the friend or relative to be sure that he or she will agree to this.

¶1308 Other Types of Assets

There may be other types of assets that bear special consideration. These would include book royalties, airplanes, boats (a boat that is registered with the Coast Guard rather than the Department of Motor Vehicles), art objects of significant value, and various unusual types of assets that have a large value.

¶1309 Valuation and Planning

With miscellaneous assets, the major concern is the value. Will there be a significant value at death? If so, will the items be sold to pay the tax or are there sufficient other assets to cover the estate tax and costs? If the furniture and furnishings are worth $2,000, there is no problem. If you have a grand piano that could be sold for $50,000, there can be a problem.

The second concern is how to handle these special assets at death. Are they to be sold? If so, who will sell them? If they are valuable, then it is possible to use a major auction house. Should they be left to charity? Leaving items to charity solves both the valuation and planning problems. The items will be exempt for federal estate tax purposes so that there will not be a concern as to value. It also solves the problem of who receives the item.

Before naming a charity, however, it may be important to determine how the painting, paintings, or other valuable items will be handled. Will they merely be stored and shown a few months every 10 years? Will the charity sell the item? Or will they be displayed over the years in a way you feel is appropriate?

Whatever special items you have, draft a will, codicil, or other document to carry out your desires.

Chapter 14

SUMMARY OF ESTATE PLANNING

¶1400 Introduction

Now that there is somewhat of an understanding of estate planning, how does one put this all together? Estate planning involves a systematic approach to analyzing the assets owned and planning the disposition of these assets at death.

¶1401 Reasons For Estate Planning

As has been previously mentioned, estate planning is designed to do a number of things for the individual or couple.

First, the disposition of assets at death is probably the primary concern. Who gets the property when one dies? It may go to the spouse, children, or others. It is very important to set up the assets to go to the person or people one wishes to inherit. This may involve drafting a will, living trust agreement, or other documents. It also involves looking at beneficiary designation and how title is held to various assets. Everything should be set up to go to the people one wishes.

Second, a person normally wants to simplify matters for the beneficiaries of the estate. If there were a choice of taking 18 months to handle matters at a cost of $20,000, or taking four months at a cost of $2,000, most people would opt for the latter approach. One probably wants to cut through the red tape, delay, hassle, and costs to make things as simple as possible for the people who inherit the property.

Third, saving estate taxes is important. With the estate tax rates running from 45-48%, there can be a great deal of savings. A husband and wife with $3,000,000 can easily save $600,000 or more for their children, depending on the year of deaths, by using a trust arrangement such as a living trust. Trusts, gifts, and other methods can save significant amounts on estate taxes.

Fourth, the avoidance of probate is normally a major consideration for most people. The costs of probate for both the executor and attorney can run from 5-6% of the value of the assets that go through probate. While the probate costs are significantly less than the estate taxes, large savings can still be realized. A single person who has an estate of $1,000,000 can save executors and attorney's fees of up to $46,000 by avoiding probate. In addition, there are some time delays and hassles that also can be avoided.

Fifth and last, is the avoidance of problems upon incapacity. While a living trust avoids problems with regard to the assets in the living trust, what about other matters? If nothing has been done, a conservatorship may be necessary, with large legal costs and difficulties.

Virtually everyone should have a durable power of attorney to avoid legal problems, even if the person has a living trust. A durable power of attorney for health care decisions is needed to cut through potential medical problems and medical decisions if incapacitated.

¶1402 Steps in Estate Planning

The steps involved in estate planning are fairly simple.

The *first* step is to obtain information regarding the person or couple's assets. This involves making a detailed list of assets the person or couple owns. In addition, a current fair market value would be listed for each asset. Additionally, it is important to determine exactly (not by guessing) how title is held to various assets and the primary and secondary beneficiaries for life insurance, employee benefits, and other assets where a beneficiary can be named.

Second, determine the estate tax and probate costs at the death of each spouse and upon the death of the surviving spouse, or if a single person, upon that person's death. How much estate tax and probate costs will be paid? This may be an estimate in view of the changing federal estate tax exemption. Also, who receives the various assets? What does the will or trust state? Who are beneficiaries for life insurance and employee benefits? Who is on the title to various assets as joint tenants? Who inherits what when person dies?

The *third* step is to determine what changes should be made in the estate plan. This includes education in determining the options and the tax ramifications. What is best for the individual? It may be a simple will or a living trust. Or, gifts may be made to children and grandchildren. What changes, if any, does one wish to make?

Fourth, it is necessary to carry out these changes. Many people are incapable of making a decision. They agonize over establishing a living trust. They attend seminars, meet with an attorney on several occasions, and talk to other people. Sometimes, a spouse dies before anything has been set up, and the options available to the surviving spouse are then limited.

Decision making for many people can be very difficult. But, no matter how difficult, people should make a decision about what they want to do.

Fifth, it is necessary to carry out ones decision. A number of people make a decision to set up a living trust or change their will. Documents are then drafted and copies mailed for review. The people never come in to sign the documents. Why? Are they afraid that if they sign they will immediately die? Procrastination is very simple but it is very deadly in connection with estate planning. Good intentions do not get things done. It is necessary to sign documents, change beneficiaries, and change title to assets. This way, things are set up the way that a person wishes.

Lastly, there is a tendency to get everything done and put it all in the safe deposit box and forget it, but review is extremely important. Documents and estate plans should be reviewed if there are any major changes, such as the death of a spouse or child, divorce, inheritance, move to another state, or any other significant event. If nothing occurs, the individual should review the documents every two to three years, to look over everything and see that it is correct or to have things changed.

Changes occur in tax laws and laws regarding trust, wills, and other legal matters. If no other changes occur, it is still a good idea to meet with ones attorney every five to six years to see if everything is still correct and set up the best for the individual. If there have been any legal changes, then the attorney can advise to the changes and what one needs to do with regard to the tax or other legal changes.

¶1403 Documents Drafted

Estate planning involves the drafting of a number of legal documents depending on the complexity of the plan and the disposition desired.

A *will* is a basic document, which is needed by everyone. A will is needed even if the person has a living trust since some assets may be missed. If the person or couple does not have a trust, then the will is needed to dispose of all assets, name an executor to handle matters at death, and name a guardian for minor children if both husband and wife die.

The will may be witnessed by two or more people,[1] may be a handwritten or holographic will,[2] or may be a statutory will under California law.[3] The original should be in a safe spot known to the immediate family and named executor.

Over the years, changes to the will may be necessary. If the changes are not extensive, it is easy to do a *codicil* to the will.[4] This is an amendment which is a separate legal document. The original of the codicil should be placed with the original will.

A *living trust agreement* or *trust declaration* sets up a living trust for a couple or individual. It is designed to avoid probate and bypass problems upon incapacity. For husband and wife, it also reduces or eliminates the estate taxes upon the couple's death.

After the living trust is established, it is frequently necessary to make changes. A *trust amendment* is similar to a codicil to a will. It changes the trust agreement or declaration without the necessity of rewriting the document. There may be a number of changes or amendments over the years.

A *community property agreement* may be needed to change title to assets for a couple from joint tenancy to community property.[5] It may also be used where one spouse has separate property and wishes to convert these assets to community property. If a couple is using a living trust, the trust agreement or declaration may have a schedule attached to it listing assets as being community property assets. If this is done, then a community property agreement may not be needed for the assets listed.

Once a community property agreement is signed, then the assets are community property. A couple should not sign such a document unless they are sure they wish to do so. If either spouse has separate property and converts the assets to community property, the assets cannot later be reclaimed or converted back to separate property without the consent of both spouses.

Even if an individual has a will and a living trust, a *general durable power of attorney*[6] is important because of the potential legal problems that may develop if the person becomes incapacitated. Even with a living trust, various matters may

---

[1] California Probate Code section 6110.
[2] California Probate Code section 6111.
[3] California Probate Code sections 6200-6243.

[4] California Probate Code section 88.
[5] California Family Code sections 850-853.
[6] California Probate Code sections 4100-4310.

¶1403

arise and legal documents may have to be signed. If nothing else, income tax return forms must be signed annually. Other legal matters not covered by a living trust may arise. This document allows others to manage the incapacitated person's legal affairs.

Along with a general durable power of attorney it is also advisable to have a *durable power of attorney for health care decision*.[7] If the person becomes incapacitated, who makes decisions regarding health care and life support systems? If no one is appointed, even though all of the nearest relatives agree about what should be done, a decision may not be legally possible. It is important to complete this document and to have it available for the agent who is named so that he or she has no legal problems.

A *change in title* to various assets may be necessary. Assets may have to be taken out of joint tenancy or, in a few cases, put into joint tenancy. If a living trust is used, title must be changed so assets are in the trustee's name. Title to some assets may be changed from joint tenancy to community property. With regard to estate planning for any couple or individual, usually some change in title needs to be done.

Along with change of title, it is frequently necessary to *change beneficiary designations*. Beneficiary designations for life insurance, annuities, pensions, and employee benefits need to be reviewed and frequently changed. Many times it involves only the addition of a secondary beneficiary. But, in many cases, a complete change of beneficiary may be in order.

If an individual is marrying, a *premarital agreement*[8] may be important to identify assets that each spouse brings to the marriage, waive rights of inheritance and potential claims against an estate at death, and possibly convert future community property to separate property of a spouse.

In a few situations, people do not want to do a general durable power of attorney or a durable power of attorney for health care. If they are incapacitated, then it may be necessary to go through a conservatorship proceeding. Who will be the conservator? If no one is nominated, the nearest relative or relatives usually has the right to be appointed by the court. If the person has no close relatives or does not wish the nearest relative or relatives to act, then a *nomination of conservator*[9] will allow the person to nominate a friend or relative to act. This nomination will come before the legal right of the relatives.

Many times people want to make gifts to various relatives and occasionally friends. The *gifts* may be outright in terms of a check or transfer of securities or deed to real property. It may be by the creation of an *irrevocable trust* to own life insurance or to manage assets for children, grandchildren, or others. If minors are involved, it may be a gift under the provisions of the *California Uniform Transfers to Minors Act*.[10]

If the person is acting as a custodian under the California Uniform Transfers to Minors Act, who takes over as a successor custodian if the custodian dies before the minor attains age 18, 21, or 25, as the case may be? Only one person at a time may serve as custodian. If the custodian dies and has not nominated

---

[7] California Probate Code sections 4600-4698.
[8] California Family Code sections 1600-1617.

[9] California Probate Code section 1810.
[10] California Probate Code sections 3900-3925.

someone to replace him then it may be necessary to go through a court proceeding to obtain a replacement. If the existing custodian signs a *nomination of successor custodian*,[11] then such a court proceeding will not be necessary.

Not all of the above occur in every estate. The documents depend upon the individual or couple's situation, what they want to do, what assets they own, and the title and beneficiary designation to their assets.

¶1404 Possible Solutions to Estate Planning Problems

The following is a summary of possible estate planning solutions to various estate planning situations or problems.

Estate Tax

- Living trust for husband and wife
- Gifts
- Outright
- Irrevocable trust
- California Uniform Transfers to Minors Act
- Charitable trust or bequest

Probate

- Living trust
- Joint tenancy*
- Beneficiary designation*
- Trustee account*
- Payable on death designation*

Incapacity

- Living trust
- Joint tenancy*
- General durable power of attorney
- Durable power of attorney for health care decisions

Financially Taking Care of Someone

- Living trust
- Testamentary trust
- C.U.T.M.A.
- Irrevocable trust

  * Only applies in certain cases.

¶1405 Basic Information

The following information and documents are needed with regard to a person or couple's assets in order to do estate planning.

---

[11] California Probate Code section 3918(b).

List of Assets and How Title is Held

- Real estate
- Brokerage accounts
- Stocks and bonds
- Mutual funds
- Limited partnerships
- Business interests
- Bank, savings, and credit union accounts
- Vehicles, furniture, and personal items
- Life insurance
- Employee benefits
- Other assets (of more than $5,000)

Financial information (for each of the above assets)

- Description in terms of legal description of real estate, number of shares, account number, or other identifying information
- Current fair market value
- Income tax cost basis
- Title to asset
- Loans against assets, if any
- Beneficiaries named for life insurance and employee benefits
- Breakdown of separate and community property for husband and wife
- Family information
- Names and birthdates of husband and wife or individual
- Names and birthdates of children
- Any people who are financially dependent on person or couple
- Any potential future inheritance of over $5,000
- Any gift tax returns that were previously filed
- Any trust in which a person has a present or future interest

Documents to Be Reviewed

- Will or wills (for couple)
- Codicils to will
- Living trust agreement or declaration
- Trust amendments
- Pre-nuptial agreement
- Community property agreement
- Prior divorce settlement if it affects any assets owned
- General partnership agreements
- Buy-sell agreements
- Agreements affecting any assets owned or business interests

¶1405

¶1406 Professional Assistance

As has been previously mentioned, if an individual or couple has much in the way of assets, an attorney is necessary. Even if the estate is modest, there may be concerns for guardians to minor children, trusts for minors and others, or other complicated situations.

Too often an attorney has to undertake probate to "unscramble" a legal problem brought on by someone who attempted to do the estate planning without professional help. Very few people who are not attorneys have the legal background to understand the potential legal problems and to draft documents for estate planning.

If the person or couple's estate plan is complicated, an attorney who specializes in estate planning needs to be consulted rather than an attorney who is in general practice and who only occasionally does wills or trusts.

¶1407 Conclusion

Procrastination is very easy. Since people work a lifetime to accumulate wealth, no matter how much it is worth, it is important to take a small amount of time to determine what to do with assets at death. Since everyone is going to die, we should accept this and plan accordingly. Estate planning can certainly make life easier, less traumatic, and less costly for the relatives left behind. Take the time and the effort to do it.

Practice Tools

¶10,001 SUMMARY OF CALIFORNIA LAWS OF INTESTATE SUCCESSION

The following is a summary of the rules of intestate succession in the State of California. "Intestate succession" refers to who inherits a person's assets if he or she dies without a will.

MARRIED PERSON

If a person dies and he or she was married at the time of death, who inherits depends upon the character of the deceased person's assets.

Community property Assets acquired during marriage by work or because of work while living in California or another community property state or country. Anything purchased with community property assets. All goes to the surviving spouse.

Quasi-Community property Assets acquired during marriage by work or because of work while living in a non-community property state or country. Anything purchased with quasi-community property. All goes to surviving spouse.

Separate property Assets owned by a married person at the time of marriage or later acquired by way of gift or inheritance. All earnings and appreciation from separate property. Divided between spouse and others as follows:

- **Spouse and One Child of the Deceased:** One-half (1/2) to spouse and one-half (1/2) to child.

- **Spouse and Two or More Children of the Deceased:** One-third (1/3) to spouse and two-thirds (2/3) to children. Children's shares divided equally. If a child of the deceased is also dead, but has children, the share due that child goes to his or her children in equal shares.

- **Spouse and Parents of the Deceased (no children):** One-half (1/2) to spouse and one-half (1/2) to deceased's parents, equally. If one parent is deceased, all of the one-half (1/2) goes to the surviving parent.

- **Spouse and Brothers and Sisters of the Deceased (no children or parents):** Half-brothers and sisters of the deceased are treated the same as full-brothers and sisters. One-half (1/2) to spouse and one half (1/2) to brothers and sisters. Brothers and sisters shares are divided equally. If any brothers or sisters are deceased but have children, the deceased brother's or sister's share goes to his or her children equally.

- **Spouse, but no Children, Grandchildren, Parents, Brothers, Sisters, Nephews or Nieces of the Deceased:** All to spouse.

SINGLE PERSON

The following relatives inherit in the order listed:

- Children equally. If any child is deceased, but had children, the deceased child's share is divided equally among his or her children
- Parents, or the surviving parent if one is deceased.
- Brothers and sisters equally, including half-brothers and sisters. If any are deceased, the children of the deceased brother or sister receive that parent's share
- Grandparents equally. If none living, then to their decedents, such as uncles, aunts and cousins.
- Children and grandchildren of a predeceased spouse.
- Next of kin, or nearest blood relative.
- Parents of a predeceased spouse.
- Brothers and sisters of a predeceased spouse, with children of a deceased brother and sister taking that parent's share.
- State of California.

SPECIAL RULES

If the decedent is survived by a "domestic partner," which partnership has been registered with the California Secretary of State and not revoked prior to death, the surviving partner inherits the same as a spouse inheriting separate property of a decedent. Depending on the relatives who survive, the Domestic Partner receives one-half, one-third, or all of the deceased partner's assets.

The terms "child" and "children" include anyone born to or adopted by a person. The marital status of the parents does not affect the rights of inheritance. In addition a person may be a "child" of the deceased and inherit if the person was a stepchild, foster child, or was adopted by another person. California Probate Code Sections 6450-6455 set forth the rather complicated rules.

If a person is unmarried at the time of death, has no children or grandchildren and had previously inherited assets from a predeceased spouse, those assets go back to the predeceased spouse's relatives.

If real estate has been inherited and the spouses die within 15 years, the real estate goes back to the pre-deceased spouse's nearest relatives. The same rule also applies to personal property (everything other that real property), if the spouses die within a five year period.

There is a 120 hour survival period for intestate succession, so that the rules of intestate succession are not determined until 120 hours after the deceased person's death.

¶10,002 CALIFORNIA STATUTORY FEE SCHEDULE

The compensation paid to an executor or administrator for his or her services in handling an estate and the fee to the attorney who handles the probate are set by law in California. The same fee is paid to the executor and attorney. The

¶10,002

compensation is based on the gross value of assets which go through the probate process. Liabilities are disregarded in computing this fee.

Assets which do not go through probate such as joint tenancy assets, life insurance, employee benefits, assets in a living trust, trustee bank accounts, and assets subject to a payable on death or transfer on death registration are not subject to fees.

The compensation is paid at the conclusion of probate, upon order of the court. It is based on a percentage of the value of the assets, which declines as the size of the estate increases.

A "fee base" is used, which is the value of the assets as shown on the probate inventory, together with income such as dividends and interest which come in during probate, any capital gains on the sale of estate assets, minus any capital losses on the sale of estate assets.

The percentages are:

On the first $ 100,000	@ 4% = $ 4,000
On the next $ 100,000	@ 3% = $ 4,000
On the next $ 800,000	@ 2% = $16,000
On the next $9,000,000	@ 1% = $90,000

Between $10,000,000 and $25,000,000 the fee is 1/2 of 1%.

On estates over $25,000,000, the fee on the amount over $25,000,000 is set by the court.

The fee which the executor and attorney *each* receive works out to the following:

Estate	Fee
$ 100,000	$4,000
200,000	7,000
300,000	9,000
400,000	11,000
500,000	13,000
600,000	15,000
700,000	17,000
800,000	19,000
900,000	21,000
1,000,000	23,000
2,000,000	33,000
3,000,000	43,000
4,000,000	53,000

¶10,003 UNITED STATES FEDERAL ESTATE TAX RATES

The United States Estate Tax is a "death tax" imposed by the federal government on all assets owned at the time of death anywhere in the world, based on the current value of these assets, if the decedent was a United States citizen or permanent resident of this country. All assets are taxable, such as real property, stocks and bonds, bank accounts, cars, life insurance, employee benefits, annuities, furniture, and boats.

Any assets passing to a husband or wife are exempt from tax, provided the surviving spouse is a United States citizen. If not a citizen, a special type of trust must be used to avoid tax. Any assets left to a qualified charity are also exempt from tax.

Any taxable gifts made after 1976 are also added back into the decedent's estate and are taxable.

Whether assets go through the probate process or not, they are still subject to taxation. Liabilities are deducted so that a tax is only paid on the person's taxable estate, or net worth (assets minus liabilities).

The chart below is designed to show the amount of tax payable, based on the net value of a person's estate (assets minus liabilities) at death, which is referred to under the Internal Revenue Code as the "taxable estate," and based on the year of death.

Year of Death	2004	2005	2006	2007	2008	2009
Exemption	1,500,000	1,500,000	2,000,000	2,000,000	2,000,000	3,500,000
Taxable Estate			Amount of Tax Payable			
1,500,000	0	0	0	0	0	0
1,600,000	45,000	45,000	0	0	0	0
1,700,000	90,000	90,000	0	0	0	0
1,800,000	135,000	135,000	0	0	0	0
1,900,000	180,000	180,000	0	0	0	0
2,000,000	225,000	225,000	0	0	0	0
2,100,000	273,000	272,000	46,000	45,000	45,000	0
2,200,000	321,000	319,000	92,000	90,000	90,000	0
2,300,000	369,000	366,000	138,000	135,000	135,000	0
2,400,000	417,000	413,000	184,000	180,000	180,000	0
2,500,000	465,000	460,000	230,000	225,000	225,000	0
2,600,000	513,000	507,000	276,000	270,000	270,000	0
2,700,000	561,000	554,000	322,000	315,000	315,000	0
2,800,000	609,000	601,000	368,000	360,000	360,000	0
2,900,000	657,000	648,000	414,000	405,000	405,000	0
3,000,000	705,000	695,000	460,000	450,000	450,000	0

On estates of over $3,000,000, the excess over $3,000,000 ($3,500,000 in 2009) is taxed at the following percentage rate:

48%	47%	46%	45%	45%	45%

Currently, the estate tax is scheduled to disappear completely in 2010, but unless Congress acts prior to 2011, it is scheduled to come back with a $1,000,000 exemption in 2010.

¶10,003

ESTATE PLANNING QUESTIONNAIRE FOR HUSBAND AND WIFE
(CONFIDENTIAL)

DATE:_____

1. PERSONAL AND FAMILY DATA

    A. NAME—HUSBAND _____

    B. NAME—WIFE _____

    C. HOME ADDRESS AND TELEPHONE NUMBER

    _____

    _____

    D. NAME OF EMPLOYER

        HUSBAND _____

        WIFE _____

    E. SOCIAL SECURITY NUMBER

        HUSBAND _____

        WIFE _____

    F. DATE OF BIRTH

        HUSBAND _____

        WIFE _____

    G. PLACE OF BIRTH

        HUSBAND _____

        WIFE _____

    H. CITIZENSHIP

        HUSBAND _____

        WIFE _____

    I. DATE OF MARRIAGE _____

¶10,003

J. CHILDREN OF PRESENT MARRIAGE

      NAME   BIRTHDATE   ADDRESS

_____

_____

_____

_____

K. CHILDREN OF PRIOR MARRIAGES (LIST HUSBAND OR WIFE)

      NAME   BIRTHDATE   ADDRESS

_____

_____

_____

_____

L. DECEASED CHILDREN (NAME, PARENT, AND DATE DIED)

_____

_____

M. HUSBAND'S BROTHERS AND SISTERS (NAMES AND ADDRESSES)

_____

_____

_____

N. WIFE'S BROTHERS AND SISTERS (NAMES AND ADDRESSES)

_____

_____

_____

2. <u>INCOME</u>

    A. ANNUAL SALARY

    HUSBAND _____

    WIFE _____

    B. OTHER INCOME (SPECIFY)

    HUSBAND _____

    WIFE _____

3. <u>ACQUISITION OF ASSETS</u>

    A. ASSETS OWNED AT THE TIME OF MARRIAGE (DESCRIPTION AND APPROXIMATE VALUE)

    HUSBAND _____

    WIFE _____

    B. ASSETS ACQUIRED BY GIFT OR INHERITANCE SINCE MARRIAGE (DESCRIPTION AND APPROXIMATE VALUE)

    HUSBAND _____

    WIFE _____

    C. DATE MOVED TO CALIFORNIA _____

    D. EXPECTED GIFTS OR INHERITANCE

    HUSBAND _____

    WIFE _____

4. <u>GIFTS MADE</u>

    A. HAS EITHER HUSBAND OR WIFE EVER FILED A FEDERAL GIFT TAX RETURN?
    YES_____ NO_____

    IF YES, DATE OF RETURN AND AMOUNT GIVEN_____

_____

B. IS EITHER HUSBAND OR WIFE CUSTODIAN FOR ANY GIFTS UNDER THE UNIFORM GIFTS/TRANSFERS TO MINORS ACT? YES_____ NO_____

5.   MISCELLANEOUS

A. IS EITHER HUSBAND OR WIFE THE BENEFICIARY OF ANY TRUST?

   IF YES, NAME OF TRUST _____

B. NAME OF ACCOUNTANT OR TAX PREPARER _____

_____

C. NAME OF STOCK BROKER OR FINANCIAL PLANNER_____

_____

D. NAME OF INSURANCE AGENT OR BROKER_____

_____

ASSETS OWNED (ATTACH LIST IF NECESSARY)

1. REAL PROPERTY

ADDRESS	DATE PURCHASED	COST BASIS	TITLE TO PROPERTY	CURRENT VALUE	AMOUNT OF MORTGAGE

2. BANK, SAVINGS AND LOAN, CREDIT UNION, AND THRIFT ACCOUNTS

NAME OF INSTITUTION	BRANCH	TYPE OF ACCOUNT	CURRENT BALANCE	TITLE TO ACCOUNT

3. STOCKS, BONDS, FUNDS, BROKERAGE ACCOUNTS, AND LIMITED PARTNERSHIPS

NAME OF SECURITY AND NUMBER OF SHARES	DATE PURCHASED	COST BASIS	TITLE	CURRENT VALUE

4. NOTES AND MORTGAGES DUE YOU (NOT PAYABLE BY YOU)

PAYOR ON NOTE	DUE DATE	INTEREST RATE	BALANCE	TITLE

¶10,003

5. OTHER ASSETS (LIST OTHER SIGNIFICANT ASSETS SUCH AS AUTOMOBILES, AIRPLANES, BOATS, ANTIQUES, COPYRIGHTS, OIL OR GAS ROYALTIES, BUSINESS INTERESTS, AND ANY OTHER ASSETS.

6. LIFE INSURANCE

INSURED	OWNER	AMOUNT	PRIMARY BENEFICIARY	SECONDARY BENEFICIARY

7. EMPLOYEE BENEFITS (CORPORATE, SELF-EMPLOYED, OR IRA)

PERSON COVERED	TYPE OF PLAN	CURRENT VALUE	PRIMARY BENEFICIARY	SECONDARY BENEFICIARY

8. LIABILITIES (LIST ALL SIGNIFICANT OBLIGATIONS OTHER THAN LOANS ON REAL PROPERTY)

¶10,003

ESTATE PLANNING QUESTIONNAIRE FOR SINGLE PERSON
(CONFIDENTIAL)

DATE:_____

1.   PERSONAL AND FAMILY DATA

A. NAME _____

B. HOME ADDRESS AND TELEPHONE NUMBER

_____

_____

C. NAME OF EMPLOYER

_____

D. SOCIAL SECURITY NUMBER

_____

E. DATE OF BIRTH

_____

F. PLACE OF BIRTH

_____

G. CITIZENSHIP

_____

H. CHILDREN

NAME	BIRTHDATE	ADDRESS

¶10,003

I. DECEASED CHILDREN (NAME AND DATE DIED)

_____

_____

J. BROTHERS AND SISTERS (NAMES AND ADDRESSES)

_____

_____

_____

2.   <u>INCOME</u>

A. ANNUAL SALARY

_____

B. OTHER INCOME (SPECIFY)

_____

3   <u>GIFTS MADE</u>

A. HAVE YOU EVER FILED A FEDERAL GIFT TAX RETURN? YES_____
NO_____

      IF YES, DATE OF RETURN AND AMOUNT GIVEN_____

_____

B. ARE YOU A CUSTODIAN FOR ANY GIFTS UNDER THE UNIFORM GIFTS/
TRANSFERS TO MINORS ACT? YES_____ NO_____

4.   <u>MISCELLANEOUS</u>

A. ARE YOU THE BENEFICIARY OF ANY TRUST?

      IF YES, NAME OF TRUST _____

B. NAME OF ACCOUNTANT OR TAX PREPARER_____

_____

C. NAME OF STOCK BROKER OR FINANCIAL PLANNER_____

_____

D. NAME OF INSURANCE AGENT OR BROKER_____

_____

ASSETS OWNED (ATTACH LIST IF NECESSARY)

1. REAL PROPERTY

ADDRESS	DATE PURCHASED	COST BASIS	TITLE TO PROPERTY	CURRENT VALUE	AMOUNT OF MORTGAGE

2. BANK, SAVINGS AND LOAN, CREDIT UNION, AND THRIFT ACCOUNTS

NAME OF INSTITUTION	BRANCH	TYPE OF ACCOUNT	CURRENT BALANCE	TITLE TO ACCOUNT

3. STOCKS, BONDS, FUNDS, BROKERAGE ACCOUNTS, AND LIMITED PARTNERSHIPS

NAME OF SECURITY AND NUMBER OF SHARES	DATE PURCHASED	COST BASIS	TITLE	CURRENT VALUE

4. NOTES AND MORTGAGES DUE YOU (NOT PAYABLE BY YOU)

PAYOR ON NOTE	DUE DATE	INTEREST RATE	BALANCE	TITLE

¶10,003

5. OTHER ASSETS (LIST OTHER SIGNIFICANT ASSETS SUCH AS AUTOMOBILES, AIRPLANES, BOATS, ANTIQUES, COPYRIGHTS, OIL OR GAS ROYALTIES, BUSINESS INTERESTS, AND ANY OTHER ASSETS.

6. LIFE INSURANCE

INSURED	OWNER	AMOUNT	PRIMARY BENEFICIARY	SECONDARY BENEFICIARY

7. EMPLOYEE BENEFITS (CORPORATE, SELF-EMPLOYED, OR IRA)

PERSON COVERED	TYPE OF PLAN	CURRENT VALUE	PRIMARY BENEFICIARY	SECONDARY BENEFICIARY

8. LIABILITIES (LIST ALL SIGNIFICANT OBLIGATIONS OTHER THAN LOANS ON REAL PROPERTY)

PAYEE	AMOUNT	DUE DATE	DESCRIPTION

¶10,003

¶10,004 INTERNET WEB SITES

More and more information is becoming available with the internet. The following web sites are available for additional information and forms. These sites change so that the URL may be different from those listed below.

Most forms and many explanations are set up in a "PDF" format, which means that the files have a suffix at the end showing ".pdf." This term stands for a "page description format," which means that the file or form, such as a judicial council or tax form can be downloaded from the web site into the individual's computer or floppy drive and then later printed. Even if you download the file it is not interactive, so you can only print out the form and then must complete it on a typewriter.

To read and print these.pdf files you need adobe acrobat reader. This can be downloaded free from the Adobe Acrobat site at (**http://www.adobe.com/products/acrobat/readstep2.html**).

Judicial Council Forms

The forms used in probate and other legal matters can be obtained free from the California Judicial Council web site at (**http://www.courtinfo.ca.gov/forms/**). The forms can be downloaded individually or all of the forms used can be downloaded in one package.

California rules of court can also be found at this site at (**http://www.courtinfo.ca.gov/rules/**).

Local rules of court for some but not all of the Superior Courts in the State of California can be looked up at (**http://www.courtinfo.ca.gov/forms/**).

California Law

All of the California codes and the California Constitution can be viewed online at (**http://www.leginfo.ca.gov/calaw.html**).

In viewing the respective codes, which are organized by title, merely check the applicable code such as "Probate Code" and then check search. A table of contents will then come up and the viewer can check the appropriate sections or subtitle to view the applicable California law.

Virtually all of the laws dealing with powers of attorney, probate, trust law, and other related areas are found in the Probate Code. The following is a summary of the applicable code sections for some of the subtitles in the Probate Code:

Sections		
	1500-1611	Guardianships
	1800-1969	Conservatorships
	2100-2893	Joint provisions for guardianships and conservatorships
	3900-3925	California Uniform Transfers to Minors Act
	4000-4665	Powers of Attorney-financial
	4670-4805	Powers of Attorney-health care
	5000-5604	Nonprobate transfer of assets at death
	6100-6455	Wills and intestate succession
	7000-12591	Probate administration
	15000-19403	Trust law

¶10,004

California Attorneys

California attorneys, with a list of attorneys who specialize in probate and estate planning, can be found at the California State Bar Association site at (**http:// www.calbar.ca.gov**).

Attorneys can be located by name or all the attorneys in a county or city can be located by using the Martindale-Hubbell Lawyer Locator at (**http:// www.martindale.com**)

Tax Information and Publications

Federal tax forms and information as well as general information can be obtained directly from the Internal Revenue Service site at (**http://www.irs.gov**).

The Internal Revenue Code is listed as part of the United States Code at (**http:// www4.law.cornell.edu/uscode/**). The Internal Revenue Code is a portion of the United States Code and is listed under Title 26 of the United States Code.

The California Franchise Tax Board site is at (**http://www.ftb.ca.gov/**).

California and other Government Sites

The website for the State of California leads to all departments and commission in the state and is at (**http://www.ca.gov/state/portal/myca_homepage.jsp**).

Other government sites including all states, counties, and cities can be located through (**http://www.statelocalgov.net**).

Other Publications

Other tax, estate planning, or financial planning publications can be ordered at (**http://www.cch.com**)

Appendix-Glossary

Abatement -Reduction in the amount of a bequest under a will because the estate is insufficient to pay all debts and taxes.

Accumulation -Income in a trust which is not paid out.

Accumulation trust -A trust that does not pay out all of its income.

Ademption -Specific gift under a will which is cancelled because the decedent did not own that specific gift at the time of death.

Administrator -Person appointed by the court to handle an estate where there is no will.

Administrator C.T.A -Stands for administrator "con testamentary annexo," which means administrator with the will annexed.

Administrator with the will annexed -Person appointed by the court to handle an estate where there is a will but no executor is named or agrees to serve.

Advancement -A bequest under a will which is reduced by the gifts made to that person during lifetime.

Anatomical gift -Gift of a portion of the body at death.

Ancillary probate -Probate undertaken in another state, in addition to the state where the decedent lived.

Annual exclusion -Annual amount of gift tax exemption, which is currently $11,000 per donee per year.

Annuity trust -A charitable trust which pays out a fixed percentage to a person or persons during lifetime and which terminates and passes to the charity when the beneficiary or beneficiaries die.

Ascertainable standard -Payments made to a beneficiary for a person's "health, support, maintenance, and education."

Assets -Things a person owns such as real estate, cash, bank accounts, stock, etc.

Attestation clause -Statement at the end of the will signed by the witnesses.

Bargain sale -A sale of assets to a charity for less than the current fair market value.

Beneficiary -An individual or charity who is eligible to receive payments from a trust.

Bequest -Personal property left at death.

By right of representation -Left to children, equally. If a child is deceased, that child's share is divided among that deceased child's children, equally.

California Uniform Transfers to Minor's Act -California law which allows assets to go to a minor by gift during lifetime or at death without the need of a guardianship.

Charitable lead trust -A charity is the current beneficiary and an individual or individuals receive the assets after a specified period of time.

Charitable remainder trust -An irrevocable trust where the beneficiary or beneficiaries receive payments for lifetime and the charity keeps the assets upon the beneficiary or beneficiaries' death.

Class gift -A bequest under a will to a specified group, such as "all of my living nieces and nephews." Class is determined at the time of death.

Codicil -A document which changes a will.

Community Property -(1) Title in the name of husband and wife, which allows the will to control one-half of the asset at death, and (2) property acquired during marriage by husband and wife while living in California.

Community property agreement -An agreement signed by husband and wife stating that all or a specific portion of their assets is community property and is to be treated as community property at death.

Community Property with Right of Survivorship -Form of title to real property. The advantage is new income tax basis at death. Property passes totally to surviving spouse at death without probate or other legal proceedings

Complex trust -A trust which does not have to pay out all of the income each year.

Conditional gift -A bequest under a will which is conditioned upon some factor, such as "being married to my son at the time of death." If condition is not met, bequest is cancelled.

Conservator -Court appointed individual or bank who manages assets and looks after an incapacitated adult.

Corpus -The principal of a trust.

Court trust -A trust set up under a will; sometimes called a testamentary trust.

Cy-pres doctrine -A court procedure that if a specific charity can not inherit assets, the assets will go to a similar charity.

Demonstrative gift -A bequest in a will paid from a specific fund such as a particular bank account.

Descent -Assets which pass at the time of death.

Devise -Real property which passes at death.

Devisee -Person or persons who receive real property under will at death.

Discharge -Formal release of executor or administrator by court after probate proceedings are concluded.

Disclaimer -Legal declining of inheritance by an individual, allowing it to pass to another. Not subject to gift tax.

Discretionary payment -A payment made to a trust beneficiary in the trustee's discretion.

Domestic Partner -Two individuals of the same sex or opposite sex if both over age 62 and meet certain requirements. Must register as Domestic Partners with the California Secretary of State.

Domicile -State a person resides in at time of death.

Donee -Person who receives a gift.

Donor -Person who makes a gift.

Durable power of attorney -A power of attorney which continues if the principal later becomes incapacitated.

Executor -Person or bank named in will to handle estate at death, and appointed by court.

Family pot -A trust where payments are made from the trust as a whole and not from a specific beneficiary's share.

Federal estate tax -Tax imposed by the federal government on assets owned at death.

Fee simple -Complete ownership of real property.

Fiduciary -A trustee, executor, administrator, guardian, or conservator.

Final distribution -Distribution of all assets held in an estate.

Five plus five power -The right of a beneficiary to withdraw from the principal of a trust of up to 5% of the value of the trust or $5,000 per year, whichever is greater.

Future interest -A gift which a person gets in the future.

General pecuniary bequest -A bequest of cash in a will.

Generation-skipping -Setting up assets to pass to the second generation, skipping over the first generation, either by a trust or directly to the second generation.

Generation-skipping trust -A trust which continues and skips over the next generation, such as a trust for a child's lifetime, going to the child's children at the child's death.

Gift -Either (1) a transfer of cash or assets to someone without any consideration, or (2) another term for a bequest under a will.

Gift annuity -An annuity from a charitable organization in return for a cash amount.

Grantor -A person who creates a trust.

Grantor trust -A trust where all taxable income and capital gains are taxable to the grantor.

Gross estate tax -Amount of federal estate tax, before deducting various credits.

Guardian -Person or persons appointed by court to raise children and handle children's assets upon death of children's parents.

Guardian of the estate -Person or bank appointed by court to handle children's assets.

Guardian of the person -Person or persons appointed by the court to raise children.

Heirs -People who receive assets when party dies without a will.

Holographic will -Will entirely in the person's handwriting, dated and signed. No witnesses are required.

Incapacity -The legal inability to make decisions regarding management of assets or medical decisions.

Income -Earnings from a trust such as dividends, interest, and net rents. Does not normally include capital gains.

Income in respect to a decedent -Taxable income received in an estate and taxed both for income tax and for federal estate tax.

Independent Administration of Estates Act -Provision of California Probate Code giving executor or administrator greater flexibility in administration of an estate.

Inheritance tax -Death tax imposed by some states on people who inherit property at death. Abolished in California.

Inter vivos trust -A trust set up during the person's lifetime. Also called a living trust.

Intestate -To die without a will.

Intestate succession -The people who receive a decedent's assets if he or she dies without a will.

Inventory -List of assets showing assets subject to probate and their value as of the date of death.

Irrevocable trust -A trust which cannot be revoked or amended.

Issue -Descendants such as children, grandchildren, great grandchildren, etc.

Joint tenants -A form of registering assets so that at death the assets pass automatically to the survivor or survivors. Assets not controlled by a will.

Joint will -A single will signed by two or more people.

Jurisdiction -County where probate proceedings are undertaken at death.

Lapsed gif t-An asset which does not pass at death because the named beneficiary died ahead of the testator.

Legacy -Any asset which passes by will.

Letters -Court document showing the executor or administrator's authority to handle estate.

Life estate -The right to the use of certain assets for lifetime.

Life insurance trust -An irrevocable trust where the principal asset is a life insurance policy payable at death to the trust.

Living trust -An inter vivos trust.

Living will -A popular term for a document which states that a person does not wish to be kept on a life support system if terminally ill. Not legal in California.

Marital deduction -Amount which you can leave to your spouse under the federal estate tax law. Amount is unlimited if the surviving spouse is a United States citizen.

Medi-Cal -Name for medicaid program in California.

Medicaid -Program funded by the federal and state government to pay medical costs of people who are financially unable to pay such costs.

Mutual will -Separate wills signed by husband and wife with identical provisions.

Net estate tax -Amount of federal estate tax which will be paid after all credits are deducted.

Nonascertainable standard -Payments from a trust to a beneficiary for other than "health, support, maintenance, and education."

Notice -Legal notice to all parties in an estate with regard to some action to be taken or of a scheduled court hearing.

Notice of death -Notice at the start of probate which is published in a newspaper and mailed to various parties.

Pecuniary legacy -A bequest in a will of cash.

Per capita -Provisions that all members of the group take equally, such as children, grandchildren, and great grandchildren.

Personal property -All assets owned except real property.

Personal representative -Term for person or bank handling an estate whether as executor, administrator or administrator with the will annexed.

Personal residence trust -A special charitable trust only for a person's home.

Per stirpes -The same as "issue by right of representation."

P.O.D. -Stands for "payable on death." Asset goes to the named beneficiary and not controlled by will.

Pooled income fund -A fund run by a charitable organization whereby a party contributes assets and receives earnings from the fund for life.

Pour-over will -A will which adds any assets missed at death to an established living trust.

Power of appointment -The right to leave assets in an irrevocable trust to someone at death.

Power of attorney -Document giving someone the right to take legal action for you.

Power of attorney for health care -Document giving someone the right to make medical decisions for you if you are not able to make such decisions.

Preliminary distribution -A partial distribution of assets in an estate.

Premarital agreement -An agreement signed by husband and wife before marriage defining their property rights in the future.

Present interest -A gift which a party gets immediately without restriction.

Pretermitted heir -A spouse, children or children of a deceased child not mentioned in a will or provided for. May receive a part of the decedent's assets.

Principal -The corpus of a trust or its assets.

Private trust -Another term for a living trust.

Probate -Legal proceedings to pass assets at death.

Qualified domestic trust -A trust for a spouse who is not a United States citizen.

Qualified terminable interest trust -A special trust for a spouse. Assets are not taxed at first spouse's death but taxed upon surviving spouse's death. Surviving spouse cannot control assets at death.

Quasi-community property -Property acquired during marriage by husband and wife while living in another state or country (other than California or another community property state or country).

Real property -Land which a person owns including buildings and minerals.

Remainder -Assets left over upon the termination of a trust.

Remainder persons -The people who receive assets of a trust at the termination of the trust.

Residue -What is left over and distributed out of an estate after all expenses, taxes and specific and general bequests are paid.

Revocable trust -A trust which may be amended or revoked.

Revocation -To legally cancel a previous will.

Rule against perpetuities -The period during which a trust must terminate. A trust cannot run forever.

Scenic easement -Restricting the use of real estate for conservation of public purpose.

Separate property -Property owned by either spouse at the time of marriage, or later acquired by gift or inheritance.

Settlor -Creator of a trust, who is also called the trustor.

Simple trust -A trust which must pay out all of the trust income annually.

Specific gift -Specific assets left by a will.

Split-interest trust -A trust which provides payments to a beneficiary or beneficiaries; ultimately terminates and assets pass to charity.

Sprinkling trust -A trust where the income and principal may be paid to a number of beneficiaries based on their financial need.

State death tax credit -The amount paid to the state in which the decedent lived under the federal estate tax.

Surety bond -Bond required in many estates to protect the estate and beneficiaries against loss caused by executor's mistake or theft.

Taxable estate -Value of all decedent's assets at the time of death after taking off all liabilities and deductions.

Taxable gift -The fair market value of a gift less the annual exclusion.

Tenants by the entireties -A form of joint tenancy holding between husband and wife. Not allowed in California.

Tenants in common -Way of taking title to assets so parties each own an undivided interest. Will controls interest owned at death.

Testamentary capacity -The legal ability to make a will.

Testamentary trust -A trust established in a will.

Testate -To die with a valid will.

Testator -Person who makes a will.

T.O.D. -Stands for Transfer on Death. Asset or assets pass to named beneficiaries and are not controlled to the decedent's will.

Totten trust -A financial account in a person's name with one or more people named as beneficiary or beneficiaries. Account passes at death to the named beneficiaries and is not controlled by the will.

Trust estate -Assets in a trust.

Trustee -The person, persons, or bank who manage a trust.

Trustor -The creator of a trust.

Unfunded trust -A trust which has no assets.

Unified tax credit -Tax credit allowed person at death and deducted before federal estate tax is determined.

Unitrust -A charitable trust which pays out a percentage of its value to a designated beneficiary or beneficiaries each year. Assets ultimately pass to the charity.

Widow's election -A provision in the will which requires the spouse to allow his or her half of the community property to pass by the deceased spouse's will or forfeit any inheritance.

Will -Legal document passing assets at death.

Witnessed will -Will witnessed by two or more people.

Index

All references are to paragraph (¶) numbers.

All references are to paragraph (¶) numbers.

All references are to paragraph (¶) numbers.

All references are to paragraph (¶) numbers.

All references are to paragraph (¶) numbers.

GIF

All references are to paragraph (¶) numbers.

All references are to paragraph (¶) numbers.

All references are to paragraph (¶) numbers.

All references are to paragraph (¶) numbers.

All references are to paragraph (¶) numbers.

All references are to paragraph (¶) numbers.